This book should be returned to any branch of the
Lancashire County Library on or before the date

11/14

The Big Questions confronts the fundamental problems of science and philosophy that have perplexed enquiring minds throughout history, and provides and explains the answers of our greatest thinkers. This ambitious series is a unique, accessible and concise distillation of humanity's best ideas.

Series editor **Simon Blackburn** is Distinguished Research Professor at the University of North Carolina, and Professor of Philosophy at the New College of the Humanities. He was, for many years, Professor of Philosophy at the University of Cambridge, and is one of the most distinguished philosophers writing today. He is the author of the bestselling books *The Oxford Dictionary of Philosophy*, *Think*, *Being Good*, *Lust*, *Truth: A Guide for the Perplexed* and *How to Read Hume*. He lives in Cambridge.

WITHOUT GOD, IS EVERYTHING PERMITTED ?

The Big Questions in Ethics

JULIAN BAGGINI

SERIES EDITOR
Simon Blackburn

Quercus

Hardback edition first published in 2012 as
ETHICS: The Big Questions by Quercus Editions Ltd

This paperback edition published in 2014 by
Quercus Editions Ltd
55 Baker Street
Seventh Floor, South Block
London
W1U 8EW

A CIP catalogue record for this book is available
from the British Library

PB ISBN 978 1 78087 597 2
Ebook ISBN 978 1 78087 566 8

10 9 8 7 6 5 4 3 2 1

Tex design and typeset by IDSUK (Data connection) Ltd

Printed and bound in Great Britain by Clays Ltd, St Ives plc

Contents

Preface

In common with most other periods in history, ours is a time of moral decline. At least, that's what most people seem to think. In the United States, Gallup conducts an annual poll which always finds a large majority believing that moral values are in decline, with around 38–45 per cent judging the country's values to be poor and only 14–23 per cent rating them good or excellent.[1] A few years ago, a poll in the UK for the BBC showed that 83 per cent agreed with the statement 'Britain is experiencing a moral decline'.[2]

Morality's descent, however, seems to be accompanied by the ascent of ethics. Go into any mainstream supermarket nowadays and you'll find a number of ethical products, from fairly traded food to eco-friendly cleaners. Most businesses now have codes of ethics and heads of 'Corporate Social Responsibility'. Even during the worst economic slump since the 1930s, Britain continued to spend more on overseas aid, reaching an all-time high of 0.56 per cent of GDP in 2011, due to rise to 0.7 per cent by 2013.

How can we explain this strange juxtaposition of perceived moral decline and increased ethical awareness? I think that part of the explanation lies in the remedial level of public discourse about values. Put bluntly, few of us have any idea how to talk or think about ethics. In place of lucid thought, we find only confused perception.

The perception of decline comes when people think of morality in terms of established rules and norms, particularly to do with sexual and anti-social conduct. But this is only a small part of what comprises right and wrong conduct. In many other respects, people are more aware of the impact their actions have on others, hence the rise of business ethics and the ethical consumer. To put it simply, if morality means adherence to conventional rules, and ethics means trying to do the right thing more broadly, morality may well be in decline even as ethics at least holds its ground.

Some of the general confusion about ethics and morality stems from the fact that the two terms are used interchangeably and there is no settled consensus even among moral philosophers about how each should be defined. I take morality to be concerned with the actions we are permitted or not permitted to do, almost always ones that affect other people. Ethics is a somewhat wider term, encompassing all that relates to life going well or badly. So, for example, many ethical theorists have talked about the role that contemplation or friendship should play in the good life, but you are not immoral if you fail to match up to the standard set. The biggest questions in ethics, however, do tend to be deeply moral ones, as they concern not only how well our own lives go but how our actions might seriously affect the welfare of others.

The way I have approached twenty of these big questions reflects an important aspect of ethics that emerges throughout the book. On the one hand, I want to cover as many of the major ideas, arguments and concepts in moral philosophy as possible. On the other, this is not a textbook and in any case, I do not believe that the straightforward 'Kant said this' and 'Aristotle believed that' approach to ethics best helps to develop our ability to think about the dilemmas we face, individually and as a society. Real moral reasoning requires personal engagement with issues, not a run through standard positions. So there are two competing goods: the desire to be comprehensive and objective and the desire to engage more closely and personally with the big questions. As I hope will be clear by the end of the final chapter, this reflects a deeper truth about ethics: values often conflict, not because one is wrong and one is right, but simply because sometimes having more of one good means we cannot have as much of another. In balancing these competing goods of objectivity and engagement, you'll find that I sometimes offer more detached explanations of the views of great philosophers and sometimes follow a line of argument that is my own, albeit highly indebted to the thoughts of others. This makes my own judgements and biases clear while still giving plenty of room for the perspectives of others. My hope is that, having read the book, you will also become clearer about your own judgements and biases, perhaps changing them in the light of the perspectives of the great ethical thinkers of the past and present.

Is there a Golden Rule?
Doing as you would be done by

What exactly does the Golden Rule say and is it really a good bedrock for ethics? In its simplicity and call for equality of consideration it is certainly an appealing principle. But all that glitters is not gold. Of what element is this one made?

Virtually every moral system contains a version of the same 'Golden Rule'. 'Never impose on others what you would not choose for yourself,' wrote Confucius; 'Avoid doing what you would blame others for doing,' said the Ancient Cretan philosopher Thales; 'Hurt not others in ways that you yourself would find hurtful,' is the Buddha's version; 'Do to others what you would have them do to you,' preached Jesus; and, least catchily of all, Kant's 'categorical imperative' commands 'act only in accordance with that maxim through which you can at the same time will that it become a universal law'.

Golden rules

Many lecturers in moral philosophy have told me that students usually turn up at the start of their courses convinced that morality is relative: what is right in one culture, at one point in history, may not be right for others in different times and places. Yet this piece of conventional wisdom contradicts another common observation, which is the universality of the Golden Rule. Far from the world containing a plethora of different incompatible moral values, it seems everyone agrees on the most basic principle of all.

Variants of the Golden Rule come in two apparently distinctive varieties: positive and negative. One invokes us *to do* unto others as we *would* be done by; the other *not to do* unto others what we *would not* like done to ourselves. The first tells us what to do, the second what not to do.

Interpreted one way, this becomes an important difference. The negative version can be read as a limited ethic of harm-minimization. As long as we don't treat people badly, we can do what we like. The positive version, however, covers more of our actions. It rules out everything the negative version does, but in addition it is an ethic of welfare-maximization. We need to treat people well, not just avoid treating them badly.

In practice, however, it's not clear that this difference amounts to anything more substantive than one of emphasis. For example, take how it might apply to driving. In the negative version, as long as we don't drive dangerously, risking harm to others, we can do whatever we like. In the positive version, we should do more, stopping to help if we notice someone has broken down by the side of the road, or calling the emergency services if we see an accident.

At least, that's how it looks at first sight. But you could argue that we have the same obligations in both cases. Using the negative formulation, we could say that we would not want our serious problems to be ignored by passers-by. In that sense, we can think of 'ignoring' as being something we do, not just an omission.

This is an example of a much broader issue in moral philosophy. Intuitively, there seems to be an important difference between what we do and what we fail to do, between acts and omissions. But there are reasons to think this distinction does not always go very deep and is often morally irrelevant. We do think of some non-acts, such as neglecting, as being just as serious, sometimes more so, than things which require the movement of bone and muscle. What seems to matter most for responsibility is not the *amount of activity* involved in something, but the *amount of control* we have over the outcome. I am more culpable for allowing a huge boulder to drop onto a crowd of people if I could have stopped it with the flick of a switch than I am for throwing a stink bomb which I took a lot of time and trouble to obtain into a similar sized group.

We could debate at length whether the negative or positive version is right, or whether not doing always amounts to a form of doing. But I think we can make more progress more quickly if we simply interpret either version according to the spirit that seems to be behind them. This is what we might call the ethos of reciprocal demand. What we demand from others we should be willing to grant to them in return. Some of these demands are for non-interference, others are for help in certain circumstances and so on.

How do we determine what these demands are? Not by simply jumping to conclusions on the basis of what we immediately think we would want from others. Rather, we need to engage in a to-and-fro between perspectives, our own and that of other people. For instance, imagine what the ethos of reciprocal demand would say about help for the poor. At first sight, it might seem to the affluent as though, if they were poor, they would want richer people to share half their wealth with them. But under the Golden Rule, the mere fact that people would want something does not make it a moral imperative to oblige them. Many people might just want whatever best suits them, fair or not. As a poor person, for example, I might want wealthy people to give me almost all their money, not just half of it. So we have to ask what it is reasonable to want. To help determine what that is, the poor also have a responsibility to ask what they would want if they were affluent. They would probably admit that they would not want to divide their wealth equally with people they did not know and who did not earn it. So taking both perspectives into account, the ethos of reciprocal demand would probably settle on a view that it is reasonable to want the more affluent to make at least modest sacrifices to greatly improve the plight of the poor, but not to treat their personal wealth as a public good to be divided between everyone equally. On reflection, then, to do as you would be done by is to be generous, but not to do what maximizes the gain to the poor.

Of course, you might not agree with this conclusion. And that points to a major problem with the Golden Rule: it simply isn't true that one person would choose to be treated the same way by another. Much depends on what other values you hold, other than the Golden Rule. So, for example, if you have strong economic egalitarian convictions, you might well conclude that the Golden Rule demands you do share your wealth equally with others. That's what you would expect if the boot was on the other foot. If, on the other hand, you believe in individual liberty to pursue wealth, you might think, without any self-delusion, that if you were poor, you would not expect the wealthy to share their money with you equally. You might in some way *want* them to do so, but only in the same way you might want a dying eccentric to leave you all their money in their will: it's a desire, but you would not think it a reasonable foundation on which to base an expectation or a moral imperative.

To sum up, the first major problem with the Golden Rule is that we can't use it to generate a moral command on the basis of what we want or desire from other people. Instead we have to think of what it would be reasonable to ask of others. But as soon as we do this, we have to invoke, at least implicitly, certain values that state what is fair, just or reasonable – and there are many different, incompatible values we might choose, such as distributing wealth on the basis of need or reward for achievement. So the Golden Rule doesn't actually generate a universal ethic. The best it seems to offer is a kind of universal test for whether a value we hold is consistent: does it fit the ethos of reciprocal demand? That might whittle down the number of possible things that we might do, but it leaves open a wide range of options. Because not everyone has the same idea of how they should be treated by others, not everyone will be led by the Golden Rule to the same moral maxims.

The demands of consistency

Could it then be that the Golden Rule is actually a meta-rule, a rule about rules? What it says is that you may not have one rule for yourself and another for someone else. Consistency demands that you expect yourself to follow the same rules as you require others to follow, and they to follow the ones you do. On what exactly these rules are, however, the Golden Rule is silent.

The consistency requirement would still be powerful even if it only gave us a binding reason to be moral. The question 'why be good?' is a difficult one to answer, and the Golden Rule promises an answer that requires no more than a recognition of the claims of logical coherence and consistency. No one did more to pursue this as a basis for morality than Immanuel Kant, who thought that reason alone could generate the command to treat others as yourself.

Let's start with a specific example. Kant asks, 'May I, when hard pressed, make a promise with the intention not to keep it?'[3] Kant suggests that the way to answer this is to ask yourself the question parents perennially pose to their naughty offspring: 'How would you like it if everyone else behaved like that?' Or, as Kant put it, 'Should I be content that my maxim (to extricate myself from difficulty by a false promise) should hold good as a universal law, for myself as well as for others?' Can I in all consistency assent that 'Every one may make a deceitful promise when he finds himself in a difficulty from which he cannot otherwise extricate himself'? Kant says I cannot:

> *For with such a law there would be no promises at all, since it would be in vain to allege my intention in regard to my future actions to those who would not believe this allegation, or if they over hastily did so would pay me back in my own coin. Hence my maxim, as soon as it should be made a universal law, would necessarily destroy itself.*

Simply imagining what would happen if something you permitted yourself to do became a universal law allows us to see that some actions are just illogical. Lying, and other moral wrongs, are thus ruled out by the pure use of reason alone, irrespective of what you may desire or what serves your immediate interest. You may want to lie and you might benefit from telling a particular lie, but reason shows lie-telling cannot be a universal moral law and so you are wrong to do it.

The big question is why should we be bothered about whether something would work as a universal law. Passing a sign saying 'do not walk on the grass', for example, I can see that if everyone walked on the grass the lawn would be ruined. But if no one is around to be led astray by my example and it helps me to cut across, why not? Isn't the answer to 'what if everyone did it?' sometimes 'but not everyone will'?

Many philosophers since Kant have tried to address this problem. One is John Searle, who argued that there are 'rationally binding desire-independent altruistic reasons for action.'[4] This is a bit of a mouthful, but the core idea is not as complicated as it sounds. Using the example of pain, Searle's argument starts by claiming that we cannot say 'I am in pain' without accepting that others in similar situations would also be in pain. We then see that our pain creates a need for help. My need for help is thus a reason for other people to help me. But if that is true in my case, then if someone else is in pain, that too creates a need for help, one which creates a reason for me to help them. So independently of what I desire or do not desire, I have to recognize that there are reasons why I should help others. All this arises, simply, from a recognition of what consistency demands.

I think Searle's argument fails because his claim that my pain creates a reason for you to help does not tell us for whom it is a reason.[5] So, while it is undoubtedly true that merely being in pain is a reason *for me* for you to help me, it does not follow that it must be a reason *for you* for you to help me. Even to the extent that it does provide some kind of reason for you to help, it is not the kind of reason that implies moral obligation. Half-price carrots at the market is a reason for me to shop there, but it is not a compelling one, if I don't like or need carrots. At any one time I have a large number of needs: I need to lose weight, get to the train station on time, have some lunch, take my medicine and so on. In Searle's view, all these needs must create reasons for others to help me. But this cannot mean that other people are somehow morally obliged to help me. If it did, we would all be morally obliged to help other people meet any need they have. That is a *reductio ad absurdum* of Searle's argument: it shows that, taken to its logical conclusion, it ends up in absurdity, which shows us that there must be something wrong with it.

The more general problem is that there is always a logical gap between recognizing that there is a reason *for me* for you to behave morally and concluding that this means there is a reason *for you* for you to behave morally. Because there is no inconsistency between accepting that a reason of the first kind is not a reason of the second, we cannot generate, from the demands of consistency alone, universal moral laws or obligations.

Nonetheless, if we give up the idea that moral laws can be generated by the application of pure logic alone we can still get some use out of the demand of consistency. Rather than claiming that logic demands consistency, we could instead appeal to a principle of reasonableness: it is not reasonable to apply one rule to some and another to others if there are no morally relevant differences between their two situations. Differential treatment or condemnation would be arbitrary and unjustified. Now, if you want to turn around and argue that there is no *logical* inconsistency in having one rule for yourself and another for everyone else, I would not argue with you. I would simply say that I am not concerned with pure logic but ethics and reasonableness. All sorts of things are reasonable by the lights of rationality without being logically necessary. It is reasonable, for example, to think that eating a lot of saturated fat is bad for you, but it would be too much to claim that we have rationally proved that that must always be the case. It is possible that we will yet discover that saturated fat is merely correlated with bad health and that other things that tend to be eaten alongside it cause the health damage.

If we accept this we are still faced with the difficult question of determining what the morally relevant differences are. And this is perhaps another key reason why the Golden Rule has less power than at first appears. No one thinks that it means treating people literally alike, irrespective of their particular situations and needs. An infant would not appreciate being fed like an athlete, and nor would a child like to be left as autonomous as a grown adult. In addition to generic differences between types of people, we also find ourselves in different situations and we have different needs. The Golden Rule has to allow for the fact that all these differences may give us reasons to treat others differently from how we would like to be treated ourselves. And so we need something like the Platinum Rule to supplement it: only morally relevant differences justify morally different treatment. But then, alas, we find it is precisely because people do not agree on what differences are morally relevant that all sorts of issues are unresolved.

Tarnished gold

The Golden Rule is not useless, but it is not as useful or informative as it often appears. As a crude rule of thumb, it can be seen as a reminder, an invitation to look at things more objectively, taking into account the perspectives, needs and desires of others as well as ourselves. In that sense, it is a call to empathy, which psychologists believe is essential for moral reasoning. It is also a warning that it is not reasonable to make arbitrary distinctions between people, or make self-serving exceptions to moral rules. In all these respects, the Golden Rule has a value, which is why it is quite right to have versions of it emblazoned on tea towels and included in collections of inspirational quotes. However, the idea that it provides a universal basis for a substantive morality just doesn't fly. That is why, despite the fact that everyone seems to agree on a need for the Golden Rule, we still don't agree about how we should actually live.

Do the ends justify the means?
Doing wrong for the sake of what is right

The vice-president of a developed Western democracy once ordered the killing of hundreds of innocent civilians. What's more, he kept his job, never recanted his decisions and is still a free man. Why? Because he, and many others, thought that these extreme means were justified by the important end they served. If I were to tell you that politician was Dick Cheney, the country was the USA and the date of the order was 11 September 2001, things might start to make more sense.

Cheney had found out that two planes had been used as missiles in an attack on the World Trade Center in New York. It appeared that thousands had already been killed or were soon to die. Cheney then faced a terrible decision. What if other planes had also been hijacked and were to be used in the same way – as in fact two had? Should he give the order to shoot them down, killing the innocent civilians on board, or let them be flown into buildings, killing both the passengers and people on the ground?

In fact, Cheney did not seem to find the choice agonizing at all. 'Frankly, I didn't pause to think about it very much,' he told Fox News a decade later. 'Once one of those aircraft was hijacked, it was a weapon. . . . I saw it as part of my responsibility.'[6] Looked at in some lights, his decision does look like a no-brainer. If he doesn't attack the plane, all the passengers and hundreds more will almost certainly die; if he does, the passengers still die, but many on the ground are saved. As it happens, his order came too late and was never acted on.

Nearly 50 years earlier, other US leaders had to make another choice about whether the means justified the ends. Atomic bombs were dropped on the Japanese cities of Hiroshima and Nagasaki in order to hasten the end of an atrocious war in the Pacific. As a direct result of the blast and radiation poisoning, between 185,000 and 250,000 people died, almost all civilians. But the war the bombings were designed to end had victims who were far from solely military. According to the historian Robert P. Newman, hundreds of thousands of people were dying in the war every month, mostly non-combatants, and many from starvation, deprivation and disease caused by harsh treatment in Japanese-controlled territories.[7] Another historian, Duncan Anderson, believes that had an invasion of Japan been required to end the war, at least 2 million would have died, again, mostly civilians.[8]

Debates about the rights and wrongs of these actions depends on establishing what the facts actually are. People dispute the death toll of Hiroshima and Nagasaki, the motives of the politicians who ordered the bombings, and the way the war would probably have ended without the attacks. But they also rest on a matter of principle: is it ever right to kill some innocent people in order to save many more?

This is far from being the only moral debate in which people ask whether ends justify means. One of the most controversial, which we'll come to in the chapter *Is Torture Always Wrong?* is the possibility of allowing torture in order to extract information that could save lives. A less obvious one is punishment. Given that no legal system is perfect, is it justifiable to allow a system that will inevitably see some innocent people incarcerated, or even executed, in order that a large number of criminals can be brought to justice or deterred from committing a crime?

Our intuitions do not provide clear answers to these questions. For one thing, they vary wildly from person to person. In the case of Hiroshima, for instance, you'll find people who think that it was obviously the only thing to do, others who feel from the gut that it was evil and wicked, and yet others who are torn and confused. Not only that, but even an individual's intuitions can appear to be in conflict between two situations. For instance, some feel very definitely that the dropping of the atomic bomb was wrong, but believe that the use of conventional bombs in Europe was justified, even though the latter led to a higher death toll. Asked to justify this apparent inconsistency, many find themselves unable to do so. How then can we think our way to greater clarity on these questions?

Coming down to consequences

There is what we might call a standard approach to this issue which draws on a text-book distinction between two different approaches to ethics: *consequentialist* and *deontological*. As its name suggests, consequentialism maintains that the rights and wrongs of actions are to be judged solely in terms of the consequences that follow from them. If there are two possible actions, you should choose the one that has the better outcome. Better could mean: produces more happiness, reduces more suffering, enables more choice or freedom, promotes greater autonomy, advances the species, or many other things besides. Different theories fill out the detail of 'better' in different ways. The underlying principle, however, is that the right is what results in more of what is good, the wrong is what produces more of what is bad.

Deontological ethics, on the other hand, maintains that morality is about fulfilling duties and obligations, irrespective of the consequences. For example, we have a duty not to kill the innocent. That duty cannot be trumped by the desire to protect other innocents. So, we may have to follow a course of action that results in more bad things happening, more innocent people dying, in order to do the right thing. So whereas for the consequentialist what is right and what is a good state of affairs are intimately linked, for the deontologist, the right and the good are independent. A world in which people act rightly might contain more bad things than one in which they do wrong.

Framed in this way, the question of the hijacked plane, for instance, becomes one over which moral theory is correct. If you're a consequentialist, then the right thing to do is as Cheney did: you order the shooting down of a plane full of innocents because that is the way to save most lives. If you're a deontologist, you do not order the plane to be shot down, as that would require you to kill innocents, which is morally impermissible. The same kind of logic applies to Hiroshima and Nagasaki: the consequentialist – if convinced it would clearly save many more lives in the medium to long term – would drop the bomb, the deontologist would not.

Adopting this approach might get you a pass in an ethics exam, but it would be less helpful in actually resolving the issue – and this reflects theoretical failings too. First, if this is to work, then whoever makes the real-life moral choice has to decide whether they are a deontologist or a consequentialist. But we can't wait until we have resolved this fundamental, high-level debate before we actually make

moral choices. Given that after more than two millennia of
moral philosophy there is still no consensus over which view
is correct (and there are others besides, as we'll see in later
chapters), it seems absurd to think that making good moral
decisions must depend on us coming to a conclusion.

Perhaps even more fundamentally, I don't know anyone
outside a seminar room or lecture hall who is a pure deontologist or consequentialist. The reason most of us find the
balancing of ends and means so difficult is precisely because
we can see the claims of both positions and we don't know
how to balance them. Yes, we want to do what results in the
greatest good, but, no, we don't think that people can be
treated purely as means to an end either. The ethics text-
books thus present consequentialism and deontology as an
either/or choice when in reality most of us want to do justice
to the truths contained in both.

It gets worse. It's not even clear that choosing which
approach to take solves the problem anyway. Take the hijacked
plane. A decision to shoot down the plane could be justified in
purely deontological terms: Cheney's duty to protect US citizens outweighs his duty not to order the killing of innocent
civilians. Or you could use consequentialist terms to defend a
decision *not* to destroy the plane: although, in the short term,
taking the plane out saves more lives, it would establish a
dangerous precedent and undermine trust in democratically
elected governments not to turn on their own citizens.

One reason you can so easily justify the same decision in either deontological or consequentialist terms could be that the distinction between the two approaches doesn't run very deep. Even their most general principles can be explained in terms of the competing theory. If I were to say that you have a duty to ensure the best possible outcome for the greatest number of people, and that this duty cannot be trumped by the desire to produce any other good outcome, I have in essence defined consequentialism in deontological terms. And if I were to say that we will live in a better world if we do not make decisions on the basis of what we think will result from that particular action, but if we respect people's autonomy, fulfil responsibilities and refuse to treat individuals as a means to an end, then I have in essence defined deontological ethics in consequentialist terms.

Why, then, do the two theories appear to be so different? It could be in part historical accident. The deontological tradition has its roots in religious ethics, in which God is what we have our primary duties to. In its early modern version, as set out by Immanuel Kant, the guiding principle was not a duty but reason. In both cases, duty was framed by something other than human welfare or happiness. Consequentialism, on the other hand, came to prominence through the rise of utilitarianism, which made maximizing happiness and minimizing pain the central requirement of ethics. So there appeared to be a clear difference: in one case, morality was not to do with maximizing human welfare, in the other it was.

But that distinction was misleading. Human welfare was arguably at the heart of deontological ethics all along. Since God has our best interests at heart, obeying him was an indirect way of maximizing human welfare. Similarly, Kant's categorical imperative – the idea that we should only do what we could will to be a universal law for everyone – in effect tells us to do what is best for everyone. Utilitarianism appeared to be so different, not because it was concerned with human welfare, but because it defined welfare in narrow, hedonic terms: the greatest happiness of the greatest number. But if one takes on a broader conception of human flourishing, then all of a sudden deontological-sounding goods flood in. We no longer want only to be happy, we want our autonomy and humanity to be respected too. We would rather suffer pain, even death, to preserve our dignity as individuals than give this up for a superficial happiness. The good consequences deontological ethics seeks are therefore ones to do with human welfare, but welfare understood more broadly than simply how we feel.

If the means/ends distinction isn't one that divides deontological and consequentialist ethics, and both are equally concerned with consequences for human welfare, then perhaps it is not a useful concept to apply in moral reasoning. What makes the question of means and ends appear to be morally interesting is that it seems to give rise to paradoxes, or at least moral conflicts: the possibility of doing wrong in order to do right, or doing something bad in order to achieve something good. But, looked at more closely, these apparent contradictions dissolve. We may sometimes do things that are harmful, unpleasant, or painful to some, but either they are justified, in which case they are nonetheless right, or they are not, in which case they are wrong. In neither case is something wrong being done in order to do right. Similarly, although we can understand some actions as being bad in the sense that they cause distress, pain or even death, they are not *morally bad* if we judge they are the most ethical options available to fulfil a duty or achieve a higher good, whichever consequence you think counts. So we can do bad in order to do right – and the only reason this sounds contradictory is because ordinary speech does not distinguish the good and the right, the bad and the wrong, in the careful way moral theory can.

But if this is correct, why does it seem so obvious to us that we do face dilemmas over whether means justify ends?

Reframing the question

Let's return to our two apparently clear examples of ethical means/ends calculations: shooting down hijacked planes and the 1945 atomic bombs. My argument has been that asking whether the ends justify the means is the wrong way of putting it. The dilemmas are just as acute if you put it another way, in either deontological or consequentialist terms. Hence you could ask: does our duty not to kill innocent civilians override our duty to protect innocent civilians from attack? Or, is the cause of better human welfare best served by ending a conflict by the quick massacre of innocents or by allowing it to run its course, even if that almost certainly means more people die?

Although these are difficult questions, I would argue they have one clear advantage over the text-book versions. If you talk in terms of ends and means, you have little chance of resolving the dispute because you are inviting mutually incompatible forms of justification. So, for example, if someone opposes dropping the atomic bomb on deontological grounds and someone else favours it on consequentialist grounds, how on earth do you adjudicate between the two? The kinds of reasons offered on one side just don't have any purchase on the other, and vice versa. But if you think about it in terms of competing duties, or different human welfare outcomes, you can at least compare both options against the same yardstick.

That doesn't mean a solution pops up easily, of course. But it could help us to find where the real sources of difficulty lie; and, I would suggest there are at least three. The first concerns probability. If you shoot down the aircraft, you know you will be killing all on board, but you only know that it is highly likely that if you don't do so, even more will die: you can't be sure. Similarly, if you drop the atom bomb, you know you're going to kill hundreds of thousands but you don't know for sure it will end the war, or if it would have ended soon in any case. Hence in both cases we have to weigh up certain, immediate consequences against less certain, future ones. And it's not obvious here that we should follow the simple rules of risk assessment and calculate the likely deaths each way. Given the inherent unpredictability of the future, it could be argued that there is always a moral imperative to count certain harms and benefits more than possible ones.

Related to this is the second issue, that of clear, local consequences versus unclear, diffuse ones. How do you weigh a clear, predictable body count against the harms caused by loss of trust in leaders not to sacrifice their own people, or the possibility that, having broken the nuclear taboo, others will in the future be more likely to follow suit? Answering such questions seems impossible.

Third, the innocent and guilty, participants and bystanders, are affected in different proportions by different options. Hijackers are thwarted by one choice, left to follow their plans by the other. Civilians bear the brunt of bombing campaigns whereas combatants suffer more in other kinds of conflict. In neither case can you make sure that only the complicit suffer, but how the consequences are spread differs from scenario to scenario.

These are arguably the real, tough issues that people needing to make moral decisions have to grapple with. If that is the case, then the idea that they should instead be balancing means and ends or the merits of deontological versus consequentialist theories is not only wrong, it's potentially an obstacle to good moral decision-making.

The end of means and ends?

The means/ends distinction is often assumed to reflect a deep and important distinction between consequentialist ethics, which allows ends to justify means, and deontological ethics, which does not. If I am right, then this is something of a red herring. Even if I am wrong to claim that the distinction between the two moral theories is not as deep as is often assumed, many debates which appear to be about means and ends are about no such thing. They are about balancing things like the short term and the long term, the certain and the uncertain, clear and diffuse harms and benefits. And sometimes they are about balancing competing goods. So, for example, the debate about freedom and security is not one about whether reducing freedom is a justifiable means to the end of more security; it is about the relative importance of security and liberty.

Should we then simply dispense with the distinction altogether? As is often the case, there is an ordinary language sense of the concept that makes perfect sense. When it seems the only way to do the right thing involves causing some harm or damage to innocents, it is natural to ask whether the end justifies the means. But I think it is important that if we are to really try to solve such dilemmas we stop thinking about it in these terms as soon as possible. That means the end of the means/ends distinction, at least as an ethically significant concept.

Is terrorism ever justified?
The legitimacy of all necessary means

One reason why any defence of terrorism is likely to provoke instant outrage is simply that the word itself is morally loaded: to describe something as terrorism is, in effect, to have already condemned it. That's why in 2011 both the then Libyan President Muammar Gadhafi and his allies, such as Venezuelan President Hugo Chavez, condemned the rebels who eventually overthrew Gadhafi as terrorists: it was a quick and simple way of discrediting them.

In 2002, the international aid charity Oxfam turned down a £5,000 donation and the promise of more to come. The problem was that the cash was the advance of a book by Ted Honderich that argued the Palestinians 'have had a moral right to their terrorism as certain as was the moral right, say, of the African people of South Africa against their white captors and the apartheid state'.[9]

That same year, the then UK prime minister's wife, Cherie Blair, caused an even bigger stir, not by defending terrorism, but merely by expressing some understanding of how young Palestinians might 'feel they have got no hope but to blow themselves up'. In response to the hostile reaction these remarks created, a spokesperson for Blair made it clear that 'she did not, and never would she ever, condone suicide bombers or say they had no choice'.

In thinking about why terrorism is wrong, it's important not to make knee-jerk assumptions that of course it is. No matter how obviously wrong something appears to be, to criticize it we need reasons. Most people would think the reasons for this seem obvious enough. Take the statement Oxfam released when explaining its decision not to accept Honderich's donation: 'We believe that the lives of all human beings are of equal value. We do not endorse acts of violence.'[10]

These statements seem simple, but a moment's reflection ought to make it clear why they are anything but. The idea that 'all human beings are of equal value' doesn't get you very far because this very same principle is used to justify acts of military and terrorist violence. Palestinian terrorists, for example, will point to the fact that many more of their people have died in their conflict with Israel than have Israelis. Their outrage is therefore fuelled by the fact that they do not believe their own lives are being counted as of equal worth with Israeli lives.

As for Oxfam's assertion that they 'do not endorse acts of violence', the vast majority of us don't follow anything like such an absolute principle. Almost everyone accepts the permissibility of acts of violence in self-defence, and most will also approve the use of violence to defend innocents or bring down a brutal regime.

So, outrageous though it sounds to say that terrorism may sometimes be justified, if we want to say that it is never permissible, unlike other violent acts, we need a very good reason.

Why not violence?

General statements about the value of life and the rejection of violence are not sufficient because they do not differentiate between the different kinds of violence. So what is it about terrorist violence that makes it distinctive? To try to be too precise about this would be a mistake because terrorism simply isn't a precise concept. The most general and uncontroversial definition would be: the use of terror, against non-combatants, as the prime weapon in an attempt to advance a political cause. This covers acts of terror conducted by the state and by non-state groups and individuals, and it also covers intimidating attacks against property as well as lethal attacks.

This doesn't quite cover all instances of what would commonly be called terrorism. For instance, car-bombing a vivisectionist may have the main goal of simply killing the scientist rather than scaring others involved in the same practice. Nevertheless, the definition does seem adequate to describe the vast majority of terrorist actions in such a way that distinguishes them from ordinary military actions. Such grey areas seem to occur where there is genuine controversy about the nature of the acts in question. For example, were the allied bombings of Dresden in 1945 acts of state terror? If the aim was to frighten the German population so much that support for continuing the war would have vanished, then yes. If it was to destroy supply lines and make the German army incapable of fighting, then, however horrific the consequences for citizens, no. (It's important to remember here that simply concluding that is not a case of terrorism is not to justify it. There are unjust acts of war as well as unjust acts of terror.)

Although this definition seems broadly accurate, it does seem to shift the target somewhat from what it is people automatically recoil from when they think about terrorism. What strikes most people as particularly appalling is the use of *lethal* terror. Although for the sake of simplicity I'll usually talk simply of terrorism, from now on, it should be assumed that we are talking about the lethal variety.

So, the moral question about terrorism can be asked in a more specific, targeted fashion: is it ever justifiable to use lethal terror against non-combatants as a means to advance a political cause? Expressed this way, it looks like a question of means and ends: is there something about the use of terror which signifies it is always wrong, no matter what desirable end it might bring about? I discussed the limitations of means and ends as a morally significant distinction in the previous chapter, and I think this example further explains what those limitations are.

We can start by seeing what happens if we take a straightforward 'consequentialist' approach to the question (bearing in mind the complications discussed in the previous chapter). What distinguishes consequentialism as a moral theory is that it assesses the rightness and wrongness of actions purely on the basis of a narrow set of their consequences. Specific consequentialist theories come in various shapes and forms. One way of dividing them is between positive, negative and mixed varieties. Positive consequentialism aims to *maximize* a *good* kind of outcome. The most famous example is Jeremy Bentham's formulation of the principle of utility: 'It is the greatest good to the greatest number of people which is the measure of right and wrong,'[11] and the greatest good for Bentham was happiness. Negative consequentialism aims to *minimize* a *bad* outcome. Honderich's rather grandly-titled Principle of Humanity is an example of this: 'We must take actually rational steps to the end of getting and keeping people out of bad lives.'[12] Mixed versions incorporate elements of both maximizing the good and minimizing the bad. By adding the reduction of pain to Bentham's principle of utility, John Stuart Mill's formulation of utilitarianism achieves such a mix: 'Actions are right in proportion as they tend to promote happiness; wrong as they tend to produce the reverse of happiness. By happiness is intended pleasure and the absence of pain.'[13]

Whichever consequentialist theory you choose, it is clear that the possibility opens up for some acts of terrorism to be justified. Take Honderich's Principle of Humanity, for instance. If it is ever the case that lethal terror against civilians is a rational step (by which Honderich means 'effective and economical'[14]) to prevent Palestinians from suffering difficult living conditions and life chances, then such actions would be justified. This is the conclusion the theory inescapably demands. Similarly, for Bentham, if a terrorist campaign produces 'the greatest good to the greatest number of people' then, the theory says it must be morally right. And it is just the same for Mill, for whom terrorist attacks that promote more happiness and reduce more pain than alternatives – such as doing nothing or peaceful protest – are justified.

These examples make it clear how consequentialism allows us to answer a moral question by transforming it into a factual one: does this action have the kinds of consequences specified as good by the theory? Of course, that does not always make it an easier question to answer. In many ways it makes it more difficult. If you take as a basic principle 'killing innocent civilians is wrong', it is usually very easy to see what is required of you in any given situation. If, however, you have to think about the consequences of your action – all of them, not just the immediate, easily predictable ones – then you face the huge difficulty of anticipating all the effects and weighing up the likely effects of alternatives courses of action.

Given that the argument now hinges on a factual claim, are there good reasons for supposing that any terrorism campaign could have better consequences than the alternatives? To many this certainly appears to be the case. Take, for example, the Madrid bombing on 11 March 2004. From the point of view of opponents of Western military action in Iraq, this seemed to be a tremendous success. Some 191 innocent civilians were killed, but a Spanish government was elected which withdrew its troops from the country and so, al-Qaeda would claim, many more innocent lives were saved than died on that day. It seems inevitable that if we assess the morality of terrorism in straightforwardly consequentialist terms, sometimes the calculations of costs and benefits is going to come out as positive and we would have no option but to declare the terrorist activity justified.

Beyond the moral abacus

Terrorism is not the only unpalatable action that consequentialist thinking leads many to condone. Given unusual enough circumstances, it seems that almost anything would be justified by adding and subtracting good and bad outcomes on a moral abacus. All you need is a situation where a large number of people will be saved by severely harming one or a few. If that's the case, then you can't rule out that, however rarely, lynching, torture, rape or any number of other horrific acts could be awful but necessary – means to an end.

Consequentialists are used to this charge and there are a number of standard replies, most of which are variations on the idea that consequentialism itself provides grounds for ruling out some kinds of action as ones we should never do. In its standard formulation, consequentialism tells us what we can and cannot do on a case-by-case basis. But there are various reasons for thinking that it is difficult and/or dangerous to try to make moral decisions this way and that instead, we need to follow at least some general rules, even if specific cases appear to require we break them.

One such reason is unpredictability. Actions have unintended and unforeseen consequences, but human beings tend to overestimate their ability to know what will actually happen. Given that, there are some kinds of action that so overwhelmingly tend towards bad consequences that we should always avoid them. Although it might appear that an act of terror could achieve a greater good, we know from bitter experience that it may well not, but it will certainly produce at least one awful harm. This kind of argument is a very powerful one against third-party military invention in foreign conflicts. Many would argue that history teaches us that such actions tend to result in disaster much more often than not, and also that generals and political leaders almost always believe things will progress more smoothly than they do. So, even though intervention might look likely to turn out for the best, and even if we can point to examples where such actions have succeeded in the past, the likelihood and price of being wrong means we should not do so.

Another cluster of arguments centres on supposed facts about human nature. If you look at how we actually make moral decisions, we do not and could not calculate all the likely effects of our actions every time we make a decision. For this reason we have to rely on having good rules of thumb and good habits: if we do want people to make good decisions more often than not, it is better to get us thinking that some acts are just always wrong than to encourage us to entertain their permissibility in any given case.

Similarly, we should not underestimate the extent to which habits and social norms influence our choices. By making certain actions taboo we ensure that most people won't even entertain the possibility of doing them. If, however, we drop that taboo, then we make a range of behaviours possible and so significantly increase the possibility that through bad thinking, out of malice or in an emotionally disturbed state, someone will do an awful thing that is not justified. Many argue against torture on just these grounds. Although in theory it may sometimes be permissible, it's just too risky to allow military and intelligence personnel to think that it might be legitimate, because the pressure to get results in certain situations might lead them to decide to go ahead inappropriately.

A third kind of argument is to expand the range of consequences that we should take into account and their relative weighting. One such way of doing this is to argue that a society that condones certain forms of behaviour is demeaned in ways that cannot be calculated and so cannot be balanced against specific good outcomes. Think, for example, about the use of Agent Orange in Vietnam – herbicides sprayed by the US in an effort to cause deforestation and drive out guerrillas, but which killed and maimed hundreds of thousands of civilians and caused up to half a million birth defects. It is argued that there is a consequence for the human spirit about using such methods that is far more serious than any good that may have come of it, and this would be equally true if it had been used much less and affected far fewer people. These consequences do not just fall on victims but anyone who even thinks about being a perpetrator: seriously entertaining the possibility of doing something awful is itself corrosive of moral character.

It's hard to pin down what, if anything, the truth at the heart of this argument is, but perhaps it can be captured in the thought that some consequences are not only more serious than others, they cannot be measured on the same scale. Take, for instance, pain. Is it better that ten people feel pain caused by a natural disease or one person feels the pain of being beaten, if the pains are identical in terms of brute intensity? I think many people would say that the former is preferable. Indeed, given the choice, some might prefer to suffer in some ways rather than others, even if that means suffering more. When thinking about what is good and bad for human beings, you have to think about what things mean to us as well as how they feel or superficially affect our well-being. Pain that comes with being intentionally violated in some way counts for more than pain that comes from tripping over, for instance.

What I find interesting about these arguments is that they are offered within a consequentialist framework. Yet, in effect, they end up overspilling and sounding much more like the kinds of reasons offered by alternative theories. In particular, they echo arguments given in the tradition of virtue ethics, which sees human flourishing as requiring much more than subjective well-being and which emphasizes the importance of character and habit. For me, this is more evidence that, rather than thinking about moral theories as necessarily being in competition, each tends to capture part of a wider truth. If that is right, the worst mistake we could make in moral theory is to latch onto one of these theories and see it as providing a skeleton key, rather than seeing it as hanging on a chain as part of a set. To extend the metaphor, some doors can be opened with just one, some are double or triple locked, and having unlocked one, you may still have others left to pass through.

Countering terror

Whatever we conclude about the morality of terrorism, I think there is real value in understanding the best arguments for terror, if only to have the best counterarguments ready against them. Given the looseness with which the word is used, it is surely the case that some acts described as terrorism have been justified. Think of attacks on property by the African National Congress when South Africa was still governed under apartheid, for instance. It is harder, however, to think of acts of lethal terror which could be robustly defended, although there are some philosophers like Ted Honderich who do so. How persuasive we find these arguments depends mainly on two things. The first is a factual assessment of how likely such acts are to achieve significant gains for human welfare. The second is a trickier ethical issue of the extent to which we can point to a limited range of fairly direct consequences when assessing the morality of any kind of action. If we think any given action is justified just as long as the effects which can be isolated to it and it alone improves human welfare, I think it is probable that at least some acts of terror will pass or have already passed this test.

The best counterarguments, therefore, do not just or necessarily dispute the actual efficacy of terrorist attacks, but appeal to more diffuse harms to character, society and acceptable norms. They depend on accepting a view of ethics where, instead of a neat moral abacus or ethical algorithm, we have to take into account a messier picture of the interaction between actions, habits, character and society.

Should we favour our families and friends?

The ethics of preferential treatment

The special treatment we give friends and families may appear to be a moral problem if we adopt a utilitarian perspective that says everyone's interests should be treated equally, and that if you can improve the world in some way you are obliged to do so. But there are other ways of thinking that do not regard morality as a duty to maximize the interests of all. If we see morality as arising out of a natural sympathy for others, out of the need of co-operation or some combination of both, then it seems much more reasonable to accept that our affection and co-operation will and should be greater with those we are closer to.

Parents will often go to great lengths in order to get their children into a good school. When places are finite, whenever they succeed they do so at the expense of someone else's child. Do they ever sit down and ask themselves who deserves the place more, their child or someone else's? Rarely, I would have thought. But these same parents may well endorse the principle that schools should consider all applications equally and not give some people preferential treatment on the basis of their family's wealth or status. Yet they will use these privileges to move into the right catchment area or buy private tuition to help boost exam grades. Surely this kind of parental bias does need justification.

Susan is the loving mother of 12-year-old Henry and Connie, who is eight. She is also a grieving parent: her three-year-old son Richard recently drowned in the bath. It's been a difficult time for the extended family too. Her brother-in-law's wife has recently died of cancer, which is why Susan has agreed to take in her nephew Mark for a few weeks while his father goes on a business trip. Being the same age as Henry, it shouldn't be too difficult.

However, as the days go by, Mark becomes increasingly aware of Henry's violent, sometimes sadistic behaviour: he kills a neighbour's dog, causes a car pile-up just for fun and leads his sister onto thin ice while skating. Only gradually does Susan become aware of what her son is really like, and eventually it becomes clear that Richard's death was no accident, and that Henry had killed him. The story's ending is literally a cliff-hanger. Henry runs away, worried that he will be sent to a psychiatric hospital. Susan and Mark follow. They all end up at a cliff edge, where Henry tries to push Susan off. In the tussles that follow, both Henry and Mark end up falling off the cliff edge, each hanging on to one of Susan's hands to save them from a certainly fatal drop. But

Susan can't hold both of them, she has to let one go. Which will it be, Mark or Henry?

Fortunately, this story is fictional, being the plot of the 1993 film *The Good Son*, written by the novelist Ian McEwan. If the denouement seems a little contrived, the fundamental issue it raises is all too real. The agony of the climactic choice is a profound clash of moral duties. On the one hand, from an objective viewpoint it is clearly Mark who most deserves to be saved. But Susan is Henry's mother and most people believe that a parent has a duty of unconditional love to stand by and protect their own children no matter what.

This situation is properly described as tragic because, however she choses, Susan will have done something that is normally considered terrible. She must either fail as a parent or allow an innocent person to die instead of the person who tried to kill her. And real life contains many versions of the same dilemma, some graver than others. There is the example of competing for school places we opened this chapter with. Or take a case of when a child has a serious illness. Most parents would spend every last penny they have, and more, to try to save them. Do they ever sit down and think 'this will cost us £200,000, which could save over 300 lives in the developing world. Objectively speaking, is the life of our child 300 times more valuable than the life of one of them?' Not only are such thoughts rarely entertained and even more rarely aired, many people would think they were fundamentally immoral ones:

the value of your own child's life is immeasurable and cannot
be traded off against those of others.

Yet it is a fundamental principle of virtually every moral
system that each person's interest should count equally.
Isn't this in deep conflict with the preferential treatment we
give to our family, friends and indeed ourselves?

Each counts for one

The moral position that presents most problems for the
special treatment of some individuals over others is utilitarianism, which holds that the right action to perform in
any situation is that which results in the greatest utility for
the greatest number. Utility can be cashed out in different
versions of the arguments in any number of ways, most
commonly as happiness, welfare or preference satisfaction.
Morality demands that in making such decisions, 'every-
body to count for one, nobody for more than one', as Jeremy
Bentham put it.[15]

What this means is that we should consider the interests
of others equal to those of our own and act accordingly. On
a small scale, this means following the principle espoused
by Jesus in Luke's Gospel: 'He that hath two coats, let him
impart to him that hath none; and he that hath meat, let
him do likewise' (3:11). If a complete stranger were to derive
more benefit from the £10 in your pocket than you would

from the bottle of wine you're about to buy, then you shouldn't buy the wine but give the cash to the stranger. On a larger scale, if you could buy yourself a large house or get two smaller ones instead and rent it cheaply to a family on very low income providing more benefit to more people, that's what you should do, even though you personally will be somewhat worse off as a result.

There is a tendency to respond to this by saying that there must be something wrong with this reasoning, because it asks far too much of us. In the examples above, for example, why stop there? I myself and the low-paid family could move into tiny flats and use the spare cash to build schools and clinics in the developing world. Yes, we will be worse off, but we won't be miserable, we'll still have healthcare and our children will still go to school. At the same time, the gains to others are enormous and, overall, our resources would increase human welfare much more this way. But how can we reasonably expect people to be so self-sacrificial?

But this won't do. It might be the case that all of us fall far short of what morality demands. This has been the pattern throughout history: whole societies have failed to respect women's rights, treat people with different skin hues equally, lived off the wealth generated by slaves, and so on. Many would agree that we are almost all failing in our duties to safeguard the environment for future generations. If whole nations have been wrong before, why not in this case?

The only way to avoid the argument's conclusion is to dispute its logic, and you can do that in one of two ways: providing a utilitarian explanation for why this conclusion does not in fact follow or by questioning the basic principles of utilitarianism.

Take the internal defence of utilitarianism first. The most basic fact we need to start from is that we do not best serve the interests of everyone equally by ignoring their individual circumstances, including their relationships to others. Parenting is a good example. When thinking what is in the best interests of a ten-year-old child, we do not think it is simply a matter of putting them with the people with the best parenting skills. Unless the parents are particularly bad or unable to cope, almost everyone would prefer, and is probably better served, continuing to grow up with the people who have parented them in the first years of their life.

What this example suggests – and I'm sure you could think of numerous others that do the same – is that one reason we have for not treating everyone alike is that no one wants to be treated routinely in that way. Would I really prefer it if everyone, including people I am close to, suddenly ceased to place any practical importance on personal ties, so that good friends would be more likely to buy complete strangers drinks or presents than they would me? The key idea here is that it is only superficially plausible to think that treating everyone's interests identically is the best way to maximize the interests of all. Far from creating a utopia this would create an alienating, impersonal world where one of the things that matters most – our relationships to others – was diminished in importance.

Enlightened utilitarianism therefore accepts Bentham's insight that, objectively, each person is to count for one and no one for more than one, but recognizes that, because we have particular relationships to others, subjectively, for all of us some people count much more than others. So in order to make things best for everyone, we need to take the individual context and relationships of each one into account and not treat them all alike.

This does not, however, mean we are entitled to put friends and family first whatever the circumstances. Partiality is justified only in so far as it is necessary to enable as many people as possible to maximize their welfare. If, however, we allow family ties to determine who is appointed to public office or who gets a fair trial, then the negative effects of tolerating differential treatment far outweigh the positive ones.

That means that many of the examples where utilitarianism seems to demand too much of us may still demand quite a lot. We could all do much more for others while still being able to give special treatment to ourselves and those close to us. How exactly the utilitarian calculation would cash out, I'm not sure. But I am convinced that it would come out asking much more of us than the vast majority of us achieve.

Rejecting utility

A second way of responding to the utilitarian argument that we need to treat family, friends and strangers equally is to reject the whole idea that we have any impersonal, abstract duty to maximize utility. Rather, we have duties that arise out of our interactions and relationships to others, and people who lie outside that network have no claim on us, and we have no duties to them, other than not to harm them by our activities.

Think, for example, of the homeless man I pass most days, slumped in the same doorway, usually just sitting there. I don't know his story but his life is clearly a wreck and it's overwhelmingly probable that whatever share of the blame he has for his situation, he can't have deserved such a miserable fate. Because of that I recognize not only that it would be a better world if he could live a better life, but that it would also be a fairer one. Does that mean I have a duty to help him improve his life and create a fairer world? I don't think I do, and I don't think many others do either. The reason for this is that to recognize you could do something to contribute to a better, fairer world does not place you under an obligation to actually do it.

It clearly has to be true that to recognize you can make a particular contribution cannot obligate you, because there are far more ways in which we could all make the world better than we could possibly do. But isn't it plausible that to recognize we could act so as to make the world better places an obligation on us to do something to contribute towards this goal? Plausible, yes, but that does not mean we have such an obligation, and trying to provide a compelling justification for it seems to me difficult. As we saw in the first chapter on the Golden Rule, attempts to ground objective, impartial moral obligation purely on rational consistency do not seem to work.

Pure reason is not, of course, the only candidate for the ultimate grounding of morality, and some of the other candidates might help explain why we are right to expect special treatment of friends and family. For instance, there is a tradition in moral philosophy of seeing empathy as the ultimate basis of ethics. At the very start of his *The Theory of Moral Sentiments* Adam Smith wrote,

> *How selfish soever man may be supposed, there are evidently some principles in his nature, which interest him in the fortunes of others, and render their happiness necessary to him, though he derives nothing from it, except the pleasure of seeing it. . . . That we often derive sorrow from the sorrows of others, is a matter of fact too obvious to require any instances to prove it.*[16]

This general idea – which was also developed by David Hume, Frances Hutcheson and Lord Shaftesbury – is that morality is based on nothing more and nothing less than our natural ability to put ourselves in the position of another, get some kind of feeling for their sorrows and pains and so be motivated to do something about it. This is not an intellectual recognition that generates a rational principle, but an emotional recognition that generates a motive for altruism. Of course, reason still plays an important role, in getting us to check whether our intuitions are correct, advising on the best course of action and even alerting us to the existence of needs we might not spot by pure observation alone.

If this is indeed the well-spring of ethics then it is quite natural that we should feel more empathy for those we are close to than those we merely read about or pass on the streets. But more natural, does not mean right. Nonetheless, if feelings are so important for morality then it might be more nourishing of our moral sense to work with them, and it may be corrosive to try to override them by purely intellectual thoughts about obligation. And in any case without a logical imperative to consider the welfare of others, at least we can see why we still have an impulse to do so and at the same time see that it is part of the same cognitive skill set that generates our preferential intuitions towards friends and family.

Another way of grounding ethics is to see it as rooted in the need for human beings to co-operate socially. This has been a key feature of work in evolutionary psychology, which tries to explain why we think in terms of what would have increased the survival value of our palaeolithic hunter-gatherer ancestors. Various models suggest that it pays to behave in ways that are typically seen as moral. For instance, honesty has to be the rule rather than the exception, or else working with others would be impossible. Reciprocal benevolence is also more productive than either being a 'dove' and being good to others regardless of how they treat you, or being a 'hawk' and always trying to exploit them. Even self-sacrifice can be worth it, from the point of passing on genes, if it helps close relatives to survive. If ethics is rooted in co-operation, then it makes sense that our strongest ethical obligations are to those with whom we co-operate most and so are in a relationship of mutual dependence.

There is a certain degree of speculation in evolutionary ethics, of course, but critics often get it very wrong by pointing to behaviours that can't be explained in terms of increasing survival value, such as choosing not to have children, as though they proved the general account wrong. But whatever the origins of morality in our evolutionary past, it has clearly developed into something richer than just a means to the end of gene propagation, and evolutionary accounts of the origins of ethics do not necessarily entail that self-interest is the only reason we now have to be good. Explaining how benevolence and altruism emerged in the past is not the same as explaining how they function now. Accounts of origins do not explain everything about the current state of a thing, just as an account of how the Parthenon was built would not explain why it is now surrounded by scaffolds.

Special relationships

As we have seen, the utilitarian perspective suggests that everyone's interests should be treated equally and that if we can improve the world in some way we are obliged to do so. But there are plausible reasons for thinking neither of these extremely demanding duties falls on us. A more rounded utilitarian way of thinking may lead us to see that the greatest happiness of the greatest number is not going to be made possible by a society that gives up ties of family and affection.

That does not mean, of course, that we should give as much weight to friends and families as we do. As we'll see in the next chapter, perhaps we do underestimate our obligations to strangers. If so, it would still be a mistake to assume that means needing to give up lavishing the special care we give to those we love the most.

How much should we give to charity?
The duty to rescue

The Giving Pledge is an initiative to encourage the wealthiest people in America to give the majority of their fortunes to charity. Some of the country's best-known billionaires have signed up, including Facebook founder Mark Zuckerberg, Bill and Melinda Gates, Warren Buffett and film director George Lucas. There seems to be an increasing acceptance and expectation, by rich and poor alike, that the very wealthy are under some kind of moral obligation to increase their largesse.

Philanthropy at such a scale is surely to be welcomed, but ordinary people cannot afford to be anything like as generous. Give away even 90 per cent of $1 billion and you're still left with $100 million. Surely the rest of us can leave the big donations to the mega-wealthy and be content with putting loose change in collection boxes and perhaps setting up a regular bank mandate to support a favourite cause?

This complacent assumption is challenged by a British citizen earning an average salary who is planning to donate

£1 million to good causes. Naturally he doesn't have that kind of money sitting in his bank account, but when he set the target at the age of thirty he calculated that was a reasonable figure to give away over a lifetime. To most people, this looks generous above and beyond the call of duty. But that's not how he sees it. Toby Ord is a philosopher and he is persuaded by a line of reasoning most closely associated with his fellow ethicist Peter Singer that most of us are under an obligation to do much, much more than we do to help others.

Let's start with some brute facts. As I write this, protest movements around the Western world are claiming to stand for the 99 per cent against the 1 per cent, the wealthy minority in our countries who together own between a fifth and a third of each nation's wealth. But, as Ord points out, this indignation is somewhat selective, since if we look at the world as a whole, many of those protesters are in the top 1 per cent and almost all are in the top 5 per cent. 'When I was earning £14,000 as a student, I found I was in the richest 4 per cent in the world, even adjusting for how much further money goes in developing countries,' Ord told the BBC in 2010. 'Giving away 10 per cent of that, I found that I would still be in the top 5 per cent.'[17] 'It's not particularly heroic or anything,' he told another reporter. 'At least half the people in Britain could probably think much more seriously about how much they could give.'[18]

Given that nearly 50 per cent of people worldwide survive on less than $2.50 a day, almost all of us are among the richest people in the world and the majority of us could give away much more than we do and still be relatively wealthy, enjoying a very comfortable quality of life. Still, if we don't want to do that, why should we?

The argument for obligation

When thinking about whether we should do more to help the world's poor it might be helpful to make a distinction between responsibility and duty. Some arguments for much more generous aid maintain that somehow the rich world is to blame for many of the ills of the developing world, and so it therefore has a responsibility to right its wrongs. Such arguments affect people differently. Some will indeed be plagued by guilt into giving more, whereas others resent being 'made to feel guilty' and will refuse to be 'emotionally manipulated', as they would see it, and become even less likely to be philanthropic. From a moral point of view however, the way in which such arguments make us feel should not be the primary consideration in deciding whether or not to on act on them.

Some arguments attempt to establish our duty without implying we bear responsibility for creating the problem in the first place. These tend to work by analogy with situations in which we would agree that innocent bystanders nonetheless have a duty to intervene. So, for instance, Onora O'Neill asks us to imagine being in a lifeboat with room and supplies to spare, while another human being is drowning nearby.[19] Peter Singer considers the case of passing a pond and seeing a child drowning in it.[20] In both situations we would all agree that the only morally decent thing to do is to rescue the drowning person. That's not because we are responsible for them getting into danger, but because the value of life is such that if we can save it at such little cost to ourselves it would be monstrous not to do so.

If we agree with this principle, however, why doesn't it apply to the premature, avoidable deaths caused by preventable disease and poor sanitation in the developing world? These, too, involve valuable lives that we could save at relatively little cost to ourselves. According to some estimates, the cost of saving a life in the developing world is around £650 (about $1,000).[21] In comparison, in 2011, the average British household spent £3,181 on holidays and weekend breaks, £754 dining out in restaurants and £772 on takeaways and premium food.[22] Just cutting back on these – not even eliminating them – would enable ordinary, median-earning households to donate enough money to save several lives every year. If we could achieve so much at such little cost to ourselves, aren't we just as obliged to do so as we are to save the drowning in those thought experiments?

What makes this argument powerful is that it does not depend upon the pure kind of utilitarian reasoning that makes much more stringent demands of us, which we considered in the previous chapter on family and friends. Utilitarianism demands that each person's 'utility' (welfare, happiness or whatever else is identified as the highest good) counts equally, no matter whose it is. If this is so, then it seems incontrovertible that if you have a choice between spending £2 on an ice cream for yourself or the same amount on life-extending medicine in the developing world, the medicine is much more effective in increasing utility. But if that is true of the ice cream, it's also true of the smart trousers, the bottle of wine, the theatre ticket – pretty much everything that you buy that is not strictly necessary for your survival. The demand of morality is thus extremely stringent: you should give away all your wealth above the amount you need to live basically, without any luxury.

We have already seen why we might reject this utilitarian line of reasoning. However, the argument for giving much more to charity we are currently considering doesn't depend on accepting any utilitarian premise at all. It simply follows from an acceptance of a duty to save lives if the cost of doing so to ourselves is much less than the human cost of the death. So the onus of proof is shifted onto those who want to say we are justified in doing as little as we do. It is they who need to show why the case of people in the developing world is different from that of the drowning child or the lifeboat.

Some of the more obvious suggestions that might spring to mind don't stand up to much scrutiny. Some would point out that there is a difference between someone dying in front of you and someone dying thousands of miles away. But while this is clearly psychologically important – suffering close up affects us more than the mere thought of it far away – it is not clear why mere distance is morally significant. Murderers do not get lighter sentences if they kill using remote control devices, and theft is no less theft if it is done electronically from the other side of the world. What seems to matter more is causal efficacy – what our actions actually bring about – and we are just as capable of saving lives in the developing world as we are of pulling people out of ponds in our home towns.

Some would dispute that our efficacy is the same, since we can never be sure that charitable donations will be used properly. Indeed, there's a danger they might be used to make matters worse, by disempowering local communities, lining the pockets of corrupt officials and so on. This objection has to be taken seriously, but note that it is not one of principle: it all rests on the factual claim that aid doesn't in fact save lives. But even those who are most sceptical about charities must surely accept that some do excellent work. So what follows from the truth in the objection is that we should be careful who we give our money to, not that we shouldn't give it. Nor is this difficult, as several websites exist that monitor the effectiveness of charities, such as givewell.org, charitynavigator.org and Philanthropedia.

Yet another way of attempting to wriggle out of the awkward obligation the argument seems to put on us is to argue that distance isn't the issue, but relatedness, which we looked at in the previous chapter. Our moral obligations are not impersonal, but depend upon our social and familial relationship to them. For example, I am responsible for giving my own children an education, but not yours. I should be at my wife's side when she is seriously ill, but not at your mother's. Members of a local community should chip in to renovate a public space, not people living several miles away. All this seems like common sense and we saw some of the reasons to support it in the previous chapter. But, again, it's not enough to defeat the argument. The reason is that, although it is true that we have special obligations to some that we don't have to others, we do have some duties to strangers. In the lifeboat case, for example, it would make no difference if the person overboard came from Islington or Islamabad – when it comes to dire need, shared humanity is reason enough to place an obligation on us to help.

There are more arguments on either side, of course. However, I doubt whether any objections can completely defeat the main thrust of the argument, which is that however much more we do we surely cannot justify doing as little as we do. Rather than try to morally justify ourselves, the best we can do is psychologically explain ourselves. Human beings are not motivated by the force of logic alone. The impulse to help is a deeply emotional one, based more on empathy than reason. In the absence of powerful emotional pulls, even the strongest argument is unlikely to move us to take self-sacrificial action. As we have seen, this explains but it doesn't justify. If, in the cool light of reason, we accept the argument that we should do more to help, then we ought to fight our tendency to let this imperative slip out of our consciousness. To do this, we might try to give ourselves emotionally laden reminders of what our duties are. Perhaps that is why to say that charities always try to pull on our heart strings is true, but is no criticism. That is what they must do if they are to get us to act in accordance to what moral duty requires of us. Emotion is thus the tool by which reason gets us to do what reason demands.

Responsibility

What of the other kind of argument for aid, the one which claims that we ought to do something because we are responsible for causing much of the suffering in the first place? Some versions of this argument are based on a naive view of economics that believes all economic transactions are zero-sum games: one person can only get rich at the expense of others getting poor. In fact, overall wealth can grow, and indeed has done so. Essentially, this is possible because of increased efficiency. If I can build two houses as quickly and cheaply as I used to be able to build one, then I will be able to produce double the amount of assets, thus increasing my wealth at no cost to others. But even if there is no necessary reason why Western wealth must come at the price of developing world poverty, there might be specific ways on which we have benefited at others' expense. Global trading systems could be unfair, penalizing the poor and benefiting the rich. Assets such as minerals and raw materials might have been extracted from developing countries for less than they were really worth, depriving their economies of income they were entitled to.

Even if this is the case, however, you would need to balance this against ways in which the developing world might have helped, through aid, trade and so on. Also, it's hard to pin the blame on any given individual. How much should you or I be responsible for the crimes of our countries, perhaps committed many years ago?

Nonetheless, I think this line of enquiry leads us to a direct source of present and individual responsibility for at least some developing world ills.

The duty to trade fair

My argument starts with a thought experiment.[23] A vulnerable person you know knocks on your door and says that
unless they get £10 to repay a loan shark within twenty-four
hours, they will be severely beaten. It just so happens you
need a big hole dug in your garden. Would it be morally
acceptable to say, 'I'll give you the money, just as long as you
spend the next 24 hours digging'? The evident immorality of
the suggestion points to a principle which, once recognized,
should seem obvious: it is morally wrong to exploit a fellow
human being by using their need as leverage to make them
work for as little as you can possibly pay them. Yet this is
precisely how we do treat many workers at the end of global
supply chains, allowing them to work for pittance in terrible
conditions, because they have no better option and we can't
be bothered to pay a little more, even though we easily could.
'Fair trade' premiums do not make goods and produce from
the developing world unaffordable. Indeed, in 2007, Britain's
second largest supermarket chain made all its bananas
fairtrade certified and I can buy one today for not much more
than 10p (¢15). Similarly, there are some top-selling, mainstream chocolate bars that are now made with fairtrade ingredients, selling at the same price as those of competitors.

Just as with the earlier argument for greater aid, it is no
objection to point to the distances involved varying in the

thought experiment and in international trade. And in this case, the objection that we have no relation to the producers doesn't wash, as we are in a trading relationship with them. Nor is it a good get-out clause to say that we don't pay these workers directly, with the result that it's the importer's business, not ours. If I contract a builder who clearly uses slaves, I am just as much in the wrong as if I owned the slaves myself, just as I am equally guilty of murder if I take out a contract on someone as I am if I kill them personally. (For more on the ethics of fair trade, see the chapter *Is Free Trade Fair Trade?*)

It seems hard to avoid the conclusions that the way we treat suppliers in the developing world is unjustifiable. The injustice persists because of psychological weakness, not because of moral rightness. I argue this case passionately and adjust my behaviour to a certain extent, but I don't check the provenance of every item of clothing or foodstuff I buy. This weakness is natural, which may explain but, it doesn't excuse. If I am right, then future generations may look back at our period in history and judge that we were grossly immoral.

Living, not just existing

If there is something these arguments miss it is, I would suggest, that everyone wants a life that is rich in good things. The wretchedly poor wish to escape their plight, not so that they can live at a bare minimum standard and help others, but so that they too can enjoy some of the good things the more fortunate do. Something in this explains, I think, why it is not wrong to spend at least some of our wealth on things that are not entirely essential.

Nonetheless, the argument that most of us do not do nearly as much as we should to help the world's poor seems strong and compelling. It is no doubt unsettling to conclude this. But why should we expect moral philosophy to provide comfort? It's role is not to justify everything we do, but to point us to how we might do better. In the case of global inequality, it points the way all too clearly.

Are drug laws morally inconsistent?

The link between law and morality

Although everyone would expect there to be some relationship between morality and the law, it is not a straightforward matter of bringing them as close together as possible. Many things we consider wrong are not illegal, many illegal things are not in themselves wrong, and this is how we'd like it to remain. This relationship between what is right and what should be legal is most complicated and disputed in the case of drugs.

In 2009, the government's chief drugs advisor, chair of the Advisory Council on the Misuse of Drugs (ACMD), wrote a paper in a scientific journal warning of the hitherto unrecognized addictive dangers of equasy. As an example, Professor Nutt cited the case of a 'woman in her early 30s who had suffered permanent brain damage as a result of equasy-induced brain damage'.

She had undergone severe personality change that made her more irritable and impulsive, with anxiety and loss of the ability to experience pleasure. There was also a degree of

hypofrontality and behavioural disinhibition that had lead
to many bad decisions in relationships with poor choice of
partners and an unwanted pregnancy. She is unable to work
and is unlikely ever to do so again, so the social costs of her
brain damage are also very high.[24]

Equasy is not an obscure drug. 'It is used by many millions
of people in the UK including children and young people,'
wrote Nutt. About ten people a year die of it, serious damage
is caused once every 350 exposures and it is associated with
over 100 road traffic accidents per year. Nutt concluded
that, bearing in mind all its harms, 'it seems likely that the
ACMD would recommend control under the Misuse of
Drugs Act, perhaps as a class A drug given it appears more
harmful than ecstasy.'

So why does the law allow equasy but ban ecstasy? Because
equasy stands for Equine Addiction Syndrome, 'a condition
characterized by gaining pleasure from horses and being
prepared to countenance the consequences especially the
harms from falling off/under the horse'. No government is
going to ban horse-riding, but most do ban drugs that are
arguably less harmful.

Drugs policy is just one area where the law seems to be
inconsistent. For present purposes, it doesn't matter if you
think that in this particular case the laws are sound: simply
pick another example. There are plenty of cases where it

seems something which is legal is morally worse than something that is illegal, or that something which is morally acceptable is prohibited by law. It is tempting to think that the solution to this is straightforward: bring the law in line with morality. The truth is much more complicated.

Morality and the law

Most people believe it is wrong to cheat on a spouse, lie unnecessarily to a friend, cause offence gratuitously or to show ingratitude to those who are kind to us. However, hardly anyone would think any of these things should be illegal. A state that tried to control our moral lives as closely as this would be an oppressively totalitarian one. The government's role is to make it possible for us to live together as free, autonomous individuals, not to take a comprehensive view on what a good human life is and make its citizens conform to it. For that reason, government should take an interest in personal wrongdoing only when it creates serious issues around social co-operation and the protection of life.

The other side of the coin is that some things are illegal which are not inherently wrong. Most laws around driving and parking are like this. There is nothing about driving on the left that makes it morally preferable to driving on the right, and nor is there anything sacred about a no-parking zone. Laws restrict what we can do in such cases simply because individual decisions need to be harmonized in order to make our roads drivable and our streets uncongested. So it does not follow from 'this is wrong' that 'this should be illegal', nor does 'it should be legal' necessarily follow from 'this is morally acceptable'. So it is not possible to settle issues around the legality of drug use purely by settling the moral question.

Nonetheless, there must surely be some connection between law and morality. When laws are manifestly unjust, for example, we see that as a compelling reason to repeal them. Indeed, some of our greatest indignation is reserved for states that prohibit things we believe people have a moral entitlement to do, such as exercise their free speech or live their lives in accordance with their sexual orientation.

There are two types of theory that try to explain the relationship between law and morality. The first is legal positivism. This maintains that there is no necessary connection between law and morality. The legal system is a social construction and its basis and legitimacy lie in facts about culture and history. When making law, legislators base their decisions on the contingent needs of society, not by appeal to ultimate principles of justice or goodness. Similarly, when interpreting law, judges restrict themselves to what the law says and do not attempt to determine whether or not those laws are fair or just. If the law is an ass, it is not the judge's job to swap it for a horse.

The second type of theory is natural law. This states that laws derive their authority from their moral basis. When making law, legislators may have to take into account contingent facts about the current state of society, but they need to ensure that the laws they enact are ultimately justifiable by moral principle and not just expediency. Similarly, when interpreting law, judges do not just follow the letter of the law, but may appeal to its moral basis, deciding, for example, that a literal interpretation is in conflict with the law's moral purpose, and so reach their verdict on the basis of that moral foundation, not the law as it is actually worded.

On the face of it, the difference between the two is as clear and fundamental as chalk and cheese. However, just as I am convinced there are hardly any pure deontologists or utilitarians outside of seminar rooms, so I do not believe there are many pure legal positivists or natural law theorists in the real world of politics and law. At least, I hope there are not.

Imagine, for example, what a pure-bred legal positivist would look like. Such a person would not deny that moral considerations come into how we think about the law. But she would maintain that the law itself must be considered separate from morality. This, however, does not seem to conform to certain facts about how the law actually operates, nor with beliefs most of us hold about what should happen in cases where the law is manifestly unjust.

Take the institution of jury trial, for example. If we thought that legal justice simply required the consistent application of laws, juries would be at best unnecessary and at worst an obstacle to justice, because laypeople are less familiar with the processes of law and so less qualified to understand the terminology of legalization and how it should be consistently interpreted. Why then do we have juries? Surely because we think that for very serious crimes, the letter of the law is not the last word and we should rely on the judgement of ordinary, decent people rather than applying laws mechanically. A judge may instruct a jury that, given the law, if they accept certain facts, they must return a guilty verdict; but the value of a jury is that it always has the option of defying the judge and releasing an accused person whom they believe does not deserve to be punished, whether a law was technically broken or not. The value we place on juries therefore seems to reflect the fact that, although we may respect the autonomy of the law in most cases, we do believe there should be some kind of safety valve that allows judgements of what is right to trump judgements about what is legal.

Nor are juries the only ways in which we actively encourage agents in the legal process to exercise a judgement that is at least as informed by notions of morality as legality. The police, for example, always have to decide what to prioritize, turning a blind eye to certain infringements and cracking down hard on others. We also have in the UK a director of public prosecution who decides whether or not the state instigates criminal proceedings, not just on the basis of whether there is a high likelihood of a conviction, but also on the basis of what is determined to be in the public interest. This is particularly pertinent to the case of assisted suicide (see *Should Euthanasia Be Legal?*), where it has now been decided in the UK that prosecutions will not normally be brought against people for aiding and abetting murder if they take loved ones to a foreign country where assisted suicide is legal. Officially this is because it would not be deemed to be in the public interest, but more important appears to be the judgement that there is no widespread public approval for such prosecutions.

In addition to these real-life examples, we might ask what we would expect of our legal institutions if it was discovered that the only way to consistently apply the law was to do something widely considered grossly unjust. There are many obsolete laws that remain on statute books around the world. It is, for instance said to be illegal to mispronounce Arkansas while in Arkansas or pass wind in a public place in Florida after 6 p.m. Now, it may be that these particular examples are apocryphal, but even if they are, there must surely be any number of absurd laws that have never been repealed. If someone were to take someone else to court for breaking one of the rules, would anyone seriously suggest that the judge should send someone to prison, insisting that the law is the law?

Undiluted legal positivism therefore seems to be something of a fiction. What of pure natural law? In this case, it does at least seem possible to imagine someone who held that every law has ultimately to derive its legitimacy from morality. But the key word here is 'ultimately'. The link may be long and extremely indirect. Take, for instance, the example of a country that has to raise taxes and cut spending in such a way that harms the worst off and leads to more inequality. A natural law theorist could justify this, by arguing that over the longer run, the impact of the law would be to improve the welfare of citizens, even though there is some injustice in the shorter term. Given that every law is passed on the official basis, at least, that it is in the best interests of the nation, more beneficial than injurious to the citizens in the long term, virtually any law could be said to derive its authority from a moral basis.

Once you start down this road, however, it is surely only a matter of time before you meet a legal positivist coming the other way. For push a legal positivist hard enough and ask what justifies having a legal system in the first place, then surely they have to say it is because that serves the best interests of a populace. That is a 'normative' claim, as it appeals to norms or values, in this case, an idea of what is in the best interest.

So in practice, it seems to me that legal positivism and natural law theory actually describe two ends of a continuum. At the natural law end, it is expected and required that morality be invoked to justify laws and decisions by courts directly and explicitly. At the legal positivism end, most of the business of law is undertaken as though it were a self-contained domain separate from morality. But that is not because law really is entirely independent from morality, simply that it is considered more helpful, productive and consistent not to muddy legal waters with moral debates.

The moral of the story as far as dealing with a concrete case, such as the legality of drugs is concerned, is simply to remember that there is no easy translation from the legal to the moral and vice versa. We have to try to balance moral considerations with social and legal realities. What happens when we try to do that with drug use?

The inconsistency of culture

Society is not a blank slate into which legislators can write according to an abstract idea of what the good society should look like. For laws to work and gain the assent of the citizens to whom they apply, they have to be in concordance with the values and extant traditions of that culture. What might work in Japan, for example, where the collective, social life is highly valued, may not work in the US, which values individual liberty seemingly above all else.

Nowhere does this cultural dimension seem to apply more than to activities that involve high risks of harm. The strong libertarian argument is that individuals should be free to take whatever risks they like, and so nothing should be prohibited on the basis that it is a threat to personal safety. It is up to us to expose ourselves to that threat or not. One response to this is to argue that if legalization exposes the vulnerable to dangers that could be avoided, that is at least a reason to consider restriction or outright bans. Another is that there is no reason why a society cannot make a free, collective decision to put certain harmful substances out of temptation's way. In much the same way that a family might decide to keep cream cakes out of the house because one member is trying to loose weight, so society might decide to keep certain narcotics out of the country for the sake of those who find themselves too drawn to them in spite of themselves.

What seems puzzling about drug laws, however, is that they treat things of equal danger differently, and sometimes ban things which are less dangerous than things that are legal. In 2010, for example, Professor Nutt and colleagues ranked drugs on a 100-point scale according to their danger overall and at the top of the list was alcohol (72), far ahead of heroin (55) and crack (54). Although heroin, crack and crystal meth respectively were most dangerous to users, the most harmful to others were alcohol, heroin and crack. With a score of 26, tobacco came ahead of a number of illegal substances, such as amphetamine/speed (23), cannabis (20), ecstasy (9) and LSD (7).[25]

To conclude, however, that the law is simply irrational is to ignore the cultural dimension of drug use. For example, it might be thought desirable to ban cocaine in the UK, if you thought that bans can work. But to try to ban the production of coca in Bolivia, for example, would be ridiculous since the chewing of the plant leaves is a long-standing tradition.

In many countries, alcohol is deeply rooted in the traditions of the country. Britain has been a nation of beer drinkers since before the Romans arrived. France without its wines is as unimaginable as Italy without its pasta – if not more so, since the French have been making wine since the sixth century BC, nearly 2,000 years before the kind of dried pasta that is now an Italian staple became common. Ecstasy, on the other hand, was only synthesized in 1912 and was taken up as a recreational drug in the 1990s. It has none of the deep cultural and historical roots of alcohol.

It does not seem at all irrational to ban something that is new, dangerous and of dubious benefit while not banning something old, more dangerous, but deeply connected with many aspects of social and cultural life, from celebrations to the local pub. Why not try to manage the risks of dangerous traditions we treasure and avoid having to deal with the risks of innovations we don't want to embrace?

Arguments against drug prohibition based on inconsistency therefore strike me as some of the weakest, even though they are very common and intuitively plausible. By far a better argument is that prohibition just doesn't work, and that it causes more harm than good. That is not, however, an argument I'm going to get into now because it is not one to which philosophy can make much of a contribution. If that is the basis of the case of liberalization, then whether it stands or falls depends on facts best established by experts in the field, not philosophers. And that in itself points to an important fact about law and morality: when thinking about what should be legal, evidence for what the consequences of policy will be is often more important than abstract arguments about principle. When people agree on the facts, they will often find that they agree about the values too.

Do animals have rights?
Expanding the moral circle

The short answer to the question of whether animals have rights is, as a matter of fact, yes, because we have given them some rights through law. The more interesting moral question is whether these legal rights are a kind of act of generosity from one species to another, or whether animals have a claim to these rights and more, whether we recognize them or not.

In 2007, the Austrian Supreme Court considered whether Paula Stibbe could become the legal guardian of 26-year-old Matthew Hiasl Pan. The case was unusual, not because of Matthew's age, but because he was a chimpanzee. The legal proceedings were part of an attempt to extend human rights from *homo sapiens* to *pan troglodytes*. The case failed, as did its appeal, but the general direction of law around the world is clear. Over past decades, animals have been given more and more legal rights. In 1999, New Zealand was the first country to ban the use of non-human hominids (gorillas, chimpanzees, bonobos and orang-utans) in research, testing and teaching, except when in the interests of the species. In 2008, the Spanish parliament approved a resolution, expected to eventually become law, to grant great apes the right to life, protection from harmful research and exploitation, freedom from arbitrary captivity and protection from torture. Other countries have passed similar laws or regulations.

Great apes are not the only animals to enjoy more legal rights. In 2009, the use of animal experiments for the testing of cosmetic ingredients was banned throughout the European Union. Three years later, in the same jurisdiction, 'battery cages' for chickens were also finally eliminated after a ten-year phase-out. Bull fighting has been banned in the Spanish autonomous region of Catalonia since 2012 and hunting with hounds has been illegal in the UK since 2005.

These developments fit the narrative of what Peter Singer called the 'expanding circle' in a book of the same name.[26] The central idea is that over human history, there has been a gradual expansion of the things that we consider worthy of moral consideration, from family and tribe, to wider areas and nations, to the whole species, and now beyond. This expansion has met with resistance at every stage. Even in the 19th century it was common for white westerners to think of Africans and Asians as not belonging to the same species as themselves and treating them little better than objects (hereafter simply 'animals').

Wrongs of rights

It might be thought unfortunate that the issue of animal ethics has tended to centre on the notion of rights, since the very idea of 'rights' is much more problematic than its frequent and easy invocation in public discourse suggests. The very meaning of rights is ambiguous, and it can be understood in at least two ways. One is the idea of legal rights. These are rights endowed by human laws and recognized by law. Legal rights can change according to where and when you live and are often highly dependent on economic and political circumstances. Rights of access to free healthcare, for example, vary even more. Workers' rights also differ from place to place. In Britain, the 2003 Criminal Justice Act limited the long-standing right to trial by jury, and there have been several proposals since to limit the right even more.

Whereas legal rights are artefacts of the legal system that can be granted or withdrawn by order of parliament, natural rights, cannot be created or taken away by anyone, whether laws recognize them or not, whether people respect them or not. The most famous expression of this view of rights comes in the US Declaration of Independence, which asserts 'that all men are created equal, that they are endowed by their Creator with certain unalienable Rights, that among these are Life, Liberty and the pursuit of Happiness'.

I think that most people assume that we have at least some natural rights: to be treated equally irrespective of race or gender, to own our own property, to defend ourselves, to be free to believe what we like and so on. However, among philosophers and jurists, the existence of natural rights is hotly debated, and it's common to hear and read people quote with approval Jeremy Bentham's famous line 'Natural rights is simple nonsense: natural and impre-scriptible rights, rhetorical nonsense — nonsense upon stilts.'[27]

Most of the scepticism flows from thoughts about what the existence of a right entails. For instance, the Declaration of Independence talks of rights being *endowed*. Rights don't just exist, they need to be granted by someone with the power and authority to do so. Whether you believe in God or not, this makes rights non-natural, in that they would not exist unless the deity or human institutions endowed us with them. In neither case are rights simply there. Nature can endow us with evolved capacities, but not something abstract like a right.

A related question is whether a right is meaningless if there is no means of upholding it. If, for example, a govern-ment insists every citizen has the right to vote but never holds any elections, is it the case that the right effectively does not exist? Likewise, in a place where people can and do kill without fear of punishment, is there no effective right to life? If so, this suggests that rights can only be real in a social context that maintains them, which would again suggest that the idea that you are simply born with rights makes no sense.

A third reason to doubt rights are natural is that the notion of rights varies enormously in different times and cultures, and, sometimes does not emerge at all. Although it does not follow that just because something is natural, people will inevitably recognize it, there is surely something odd about the idea of a human universal that is far from universally recognized.

People are often reluctant to accept that rights are not natural because they think that if rights were *just* cultural artefacts they would be less binding. But perhaps this 'just' is misplaced. A non-natural right that is globally endorsed and upheld is surely worth more than a natural right that most people trample over. What matters for upholding rights is that laws and institutions recognize and value them, not whether they are natural or not.

More generally, there is a tendency to equate 'natural' and 'good' and to see their opposites as 'artificial' and 'bad'. Similarly, some have a sense that if rights aren't natural then they aren't real – they're just fictions we've made up. But the world doesn't divide up neatly into things that are real, natural and good versus those that are fake, non-natural and bad. Every work of art is a non-natural human creation, as is every life-saving medicine, and all are very real. On the other hand, every disease and earthquake is completely natural, yet hardly welcome as a result. Rights are therefore not necessarily any weaker, less valuable or less real if they are not natural.

If we do accept that rights are not natural, then we need also to accept that they are not ethically basic. That is to say, rights do not form the bedrock of our social morality, rather they are created to help protect it. So, for instance, because we believe it is wrong to kill except in very exceptional circumstances, we create a right to life to enshrine this in a clear principle. Because we think it wrong to steal and right to be able to keep the fruits of our labours, we create a right to property. Rights are therefore a means of encapsulating in legal principle certain judgements we make about what is right and wrong.

It's important to notice, however, that not every moral value is best translated into a right. We might think adultery is wrong, for example, but we do not have a right to fidelity. We might also think that every child should be able to go to school, but we will only enshrine that as a right if our country has the resources to provide universal education. Lying might also be considered wrong without there being a right to be told the truth. So the mere fact that we do not recognize a right to something does not mean we deny the wrong of doing it.

The question of whether rights are natural or not is still a very live one. For now, the general consensus is that they are not, and it's on that assumption that we'll continue, maintaining that they are still real and important. So now we must turn to the question: should animals be granted rights?

Animal rights, animal responsibility?

There are some who would argue that animals can have no rights for the simple reason that rights entail responsibilities, and animals are incapable of taking responsibility for their actions. Cats just do what cats do, and the same goes even for the most intelligent animals, such as dolphins, chimps and pigs.

According to this view, rights are conditional, not absolute. For example, to have a right to life requires that you respect that right in others. So, if you set out to kill others, you can expect that right to be taken away from you and that you may be killed in self-defence or even as punishment. Similarly, your right to liberty depends on your not abusing that freedom to commit crime; your right to freedom can be taken away if you do not comply with that duty. If this statement is true, then the word 'inalienable' in the American Declaration of Independence is misplaced, or at least misleading, in that some rights can be suspended if not entirely rescinded.

Following this line of argument, it seems animals cannot have rights, because they are incapable of taking on the requisite responsibilities. It's a neat argument but it seems to have a simple, glaring flaw: we grant rights to some humans who are not capable of taking on the requisite responsibilities, most notably very young children, the severely mentally impaired and people in comas. If having a right requires you to be able to take on responsibilities, then these humans should have as few rights as animals.

Not many people would be prepared to bite that bullet. But there appears to be no need to. The requirement to match a right with the taking on of responsibility seems to apply only to those we judge capable of taking on such responsibilities. For those who can't, we might still decide that they have some rights. The way in which we recognize their lack of responsibility is not to deny them any rights, but to withhold only those that do entail an ability to be responsible, such as the right to vote, marry or bear arms. An infant or a dog, in contrast, does not need to take on any responsibility in order to exercise its right to life. It just needs the impulse to keep living.

But is it appropriate to grant such rights to animals? If, as I have argued, rights are not morally basic, then the answer to this question will depend in part on what is morally basic about the way we should treat animals. Answers to this question fall between two extremes: 'as our equals' and 'as we like'. Although few sit at either pole, seeing why they don't could help us decide where on the spectrum in between we should settle.

No one believes that we should literally treat animals exactly as we treat humans, putting trout on waiting lists for social housing, for example. 'Equal' must mean giving equal consideration to those the interests we have in common, recognizing that their interests are not the same as our own. However, even with humans, we do not treat all interests equally, but regard some as more morally salient than others. For instance, it is in my interest for other people not to be allowed to hit me, to be given the best healthcare money can buy and for my books to be endorsed on national television by Oprah Winfrey. Only the first of these places a demand on others to treat me in certain ways. The fact that widespread media coverage is in my interests at most requires that no one should prevent me from getting such coverage, not that anyone has an obligation to provide it. In the case of the best healthcare money can buy, it might even be argued that I should not be allowed to purchase it, since healthcare is a finite social good that should be distributed according to need, not wealth.

At least some animals have interests, that much seems clear. But how much weight we should give to them is an open question. Take, for example, the shrimp's interest in continuing to exist. Does that place an obligation on me not to kill and eat it? It's not obvious that it does. A shrimp almost certainly has nothing like conscious thought, so is not even aware that it has an interest in surviving and passing on its genes. Indeed, you might say that talk of 'interest' here is metaphorical and that without subjective awareness of what is in the shrimp's interests, nothing really is.

The oddness of talking about animals' interests becomes even clearer if you think of how peculiar it is to talk of 'thwarting' an animal's interests. As far as we can tell, animals have no plans, at least not beyond their next few moves. How then can you thwart something which has no plans to thwart? At the very least, if you compare the interest a human has – in continuing to live, pursue projects and continue relationships – with an animal's interest in merely continuing to survive, it seems hard to see why theirs should have an equal claim on us.

The one interest that animals do have and which seems to require something of us is to be without pain. As Jeremy Bentham wrote far ahead of his time in 1789, 'The question is not Can they reason?, nor Can they talk?, but Can they suffer?'[28] (This is a fine illustration of the fact that one can be an advocate of the ethical treatment of animals while completely dismissing the idea that they have natural rights.) This does not mean that we have an obligation to reduce animal suffering as much as possible. If that were the case, we'd have to stop them hunting each other and also have to rove the countryside looking for sick animals to hospitalize. But it does suggest that we at the very least have an obligation not to make animals suffer unnecessarily. Pain is a bad thing, whatever feels it. If we agree with this claim (and there are counterarguments) then it may make sense to grant animals a right not to be mistreated and to be reared and slaughtered humanely in farming. In addition, to cause animals pain for frivolous purposes, such as to test cosmetics, would seem to fail to respect their legitimate interests in not being made to suffer. Laws in many parts of the world do indeed instantiate such rights.

However, with pain as in all other aspects of animal rights, it surely must make a difference which animals we are talking about. Pain may be pain, but it is more or less serious depending on how and when it is felt, by what kind of creature. Human beings, for example, are often terror-ized by the prospect of pain and haunted by the memory of particularly nasty forms of it. Pain that is felt in childbirth or that is self-inflicted by a marathon runner can be endured in ways in which pain inflicted by a malicious third party cannot. Similarly the pain of childbirth is often found more bearable because women know there will be a positive outcome. Our memory of how painful something was varies depending on when it was felt: the same amount of pain at the end of a surgical procedure, for example, stays in the memory more than the same amount of pain at the beginning or in the middle.[29]

To put it simply, you could say that pain becomes a more serious kind of suffering when it is not just felt *at a time* but becomes part of an experience remembered or anticipated *over time*. That is why human pain, I would argue, does count for more than animal pain. An animal that lives purely in the here and now may have an unpleasant moment, which should be avoided if possible, but as soon as it has passed, life goes on. The same is not true for humans. If, as seems likely, some more mentally sophisticated animals can turn their pain into this longer-lasting suffering, such as abused dogs who appear to become traumatized, we have more reason to avoid hurting them than we do very simple organisms whose every experience disappears unremembered as soon as it has happened.

There is obviously much more that could be said here, for example, about the claims of ethical vegans that our moral duties to animals extend far beyond not causing them unnecessary pain. What I have outlined is one way of thinking about the morality of animals that can take our thinking further. Rather than starting with the question of rights, we should think about what interests animals have and the extent to which these interests make moral demands of us. If they do, only then should we ask whether the granting of rights is the best way of meeting these demands.

I cannot see how anyone would conclude that animals make as stringent demands of us as our fellow human beings do. But it may well be the case that they demand more of us than we currently give. The moral circle may not keep expanding indefinitely, and it may contain different rings. The chances are, however, that we have not yet included within it all that we ought to with regard to non-human species.

Is abortion murder?
The value of human life

The question of whether abortion is murder is by far and away the most important element in the debate over its morality, even more than the woman's right to choose: a man or woman has no right to choose murder, so issues around right to choice only apply if you have already decided that abortion is not murder. There is no getting away from this as the central issue.

Arriving recently in Huntsville, Alabama, one of the first things I saw was a group of protesters outside an abortion clinic. 'Abortion kills' read one of the placards, tautologically. 'Jesus loves your baby' said another, and 'In God's court abortion is murder'.When I talked to the protestors and they found out I was from Britain, one said, 'You murder a lot of babies there.' 'Shame on your country,' chipped in another, before a third added 'Britain's being taken over by Muslims and immigrants'.

It's very easy for those of us who defend the right to abortion to dismiss people with strong feelings on the other side as zealots. If you truly believed that a human embryo has as much right to a life as a new-born child, then abortion is murder on an enormous scale: every year there are nearly 200,000 abortions in the United Kingdom, more than a million in the United States alone and over 40 million worldwide. When you consider how people take to the streets when even one adult is murdered with the sanction of the state, you can understand why anti-abortionists protest so loudly. If you agreed with their analysis of what abortion is, wouldn't you do the same?

The sanctity of life

The principle that is appealed to most in this debate (and also the one over euthanasia discussed in the next chapter) is the sanctity of life: that life is *the* supreme value and so can never be trumped by rights of free choice or autonomy. However, although the phrase 'the sanctity of life' is widely invoked, it seems that hardly anyone really believes in it. Only a small minority are vegans, and vegetarians must accept that, if they are to be supplied with dairy products, animals almost always have to be killed. Only a small minority are strict pacifists – those who would not even kill in self-defence – and most people believe that there can be just wars. Even though the Bible appears to assert the sanctity of life in the short and apparently unambiguous

commandment 'Thou shalt not kill',[30] this is rarely interpreted as being a blanket prohibition on all forms of
killing and is usually taken to be compatible with some
forms of warfare and self-defence. That is because the
Hebrew word *râtsach* used in Exodus usually refers to
intentional killing without cause. For a consistent attempt
to truly respect the sanctity of all life, you have to look
at a religion like Jainism, whose strictest adherents cover
their mouths in order to avoid unintentionally swallowing
flies. For almost everyone else, there is no consistently
followed principle that it is always wrong to end a life.
Objections to abortion stand on a pretty flimsy basis if
they rely on nothing more than an appeal to the sanctity
of life.

If you do not embrace a strict sanctity of life view, then
the question is always when is it permissible to end life? An
answer consistent with opposing abortion but supporting
self-defence and just war is that it is always wrong to take a
human life except when it is necessary to do so to protect
the lives of yourself or others. But what would justify such a
principle? To answer this we need to focus on the apparently simple concept at the heart of the issue: a human life.
The first question is what is it about human life that makes
it so worthy of protection? The second is when does human
life begin? As we shall see, the answer to the first question
informs our answer to the second.

The value of human life

Why do we think it so important to protect human life? There are two possible kinds of answers to this. One is that human life is intrinsically valuable in and of itself. Regardless of who the person is or what state they are in, human life is always precious. This may sound noble and principled, but as it stands it is simply an assertion, and most people can easily imagine situations in which they would not uphold it. Most obviously, think of cases where someone has suffered the kind of severe and irreversible brain damage that means they will never gain consciousness and they are simply being kept alive by a life support machine. Most people would agree that there is no value in simply sustaining the life of the human body indefinitely, if that body is no longer supporting a conscious life. If that is right, then we do not, in fact, value human life in and of itself, regardless of the kind of life it is.

Arguing from such cases can be complicated by worries people have about the diagnosis of permanent vegetative states. They resist the conclusion that this form of life is not worth sustaining on the basis that we cannot know for sure that the person is not in fact still having some thoughts and may want to live. In real life there are some cases where the irreversible loss of consciousness is a certain fact, due to the area of the brain destroyed. But even if in practice we could never know whether such a state of affairs existed, the point of the example is just as readily made hypothetically: *if* your body were kept alive but you had lost consciousness forever, then there *would* be no value in keeping your body alive for its own sake. This could be true even if you would never agree to switching off a life support machine in real life because you always thought there would be some doubt as to whether or not loss of consciousness was permanent.

The idea that the value of human life lies simply in being creatures of a certain biological kind is supported by the way we think about our closest animal relatives. If our place in the biological taxonomy is what counts, then there is a strong case for valuing the lives of chimpanzees and bonobos as much as we do the lives of human beings. Using DNA analysis, scientists from Wayne State University in Detroit have argued that *homo: homo sapiens*, *homo troglodytes* (chimpanzees) and *homo paniscus* (bonobos) should all be classified as species of the genus.[31] Others have argued the same point by moving humans the other way, as suggested by the title of Jared Diamond's *The Third Chimpanzee: The Evolution and Future of the Human Animal*. But hardly anyone thinks that it would follow from such a reclassification that we should value the lives of chimps and bonobos as much as we do those of humans, even if we should value them much more than we do.

If this line of thought is correct, then we are led to the second kind of reason for valuing human life: what is precious is not the mere existence of a living *homo sapiens*, but what that existence usually sustains, namely a conscious, personal life. That is why we would prioritize removing one human being from a burning building over a dozen primates. For all their similarities to us, chimps do not have life projects, personal values and metaphysical beliefs. Like all animals apart from human beings, they just live from day to day, moment to moment. No plans are thwarted when they die, no ambitions are left unfulfilled, apart from minor and proximate ones like mating with that chimp over there, or getting hold of those nuts.

In the days after conception, a fertilized human egg (a zygote and then a blastocyst) certainly has none of the features that give fully-developed human life its value. Indeed, even a mouse has more conscious awareness than a *homo sapiens* at this point in its development. That's why in the UK, on the basis of the 1984 report of the Warnock Committee, the Human Fertilization and Embryology (HFE) Act 1990 allowed research on human embryos up to fourteen days after fertilization. Until that point not even the 'precursor to what will eventually develop into the nervous system' has formed, and it cannot even be known whether the embryo will divide into twins. According to the Warnock Report,

A human embryo cannot be thought of as a person, or even as a potential person. It is simply a collection of cells which, unless it implants in a human uterine environment, has no potential for development. There is no reason therefore to accord these cells any protected status.[32]

When you consider the development of the foetus in this careful way it is not even clear when we should say human life starts. Can the life of a twin be said to have begun before it is even known whether the embryo will become one or two foetuses? Even if we decide that biologically speaking, an identifiable *homo sapiens* comes into existence at a certain point at or after fertilization, it might still be asked whether that is morally significant or whether we should think instead of when the life of the *person* begins.

No one denies that a foetus is alive. But if we accept that human life is valuable for the conscious life it makes possible, that would seem to entail that there are periods in the early development of the foetus when it does not have anything like the same value as a full human life. Rather, it gradually acquires the characteristics that give it such value, and at some point it has enough of them to be granted the same protection as a new-born infant. Given there is no identifiable magic moment when consciousness pings into existence, drawing a precise line between these two stages is never going to be possible. But draw it we must, or else we must give up on the distinction between the destruction of some cells and murder.

Drawing lines

In both law and ethics, there is often an unsatisfactory need to draw a line where nature refuses to provide a clear boundary. Set aside the most controversial cases for now and think about things such as negligence. There are some clear cases where someone is as careful and attentive as possible and others where they are recklessly careless. But at what point does being less than completely vigilant turn into a culpable negligence? There can be no clear abstract rule for this: it will depend on the precise situation, what the person in question knew, the resources available to him and so on. Or think about your responsibilities as a bystander to an accident. A person who just ignores a seriously bleeding person because they want to buy an ice cream is clearly blameworthy, while someone who enters a burning building to save the people inside is a hero. But at what point does an acceptable right to protect one's interests turn into a callous disregard for the welfare of others?

In neither of these cases, however, does the lack of a sharp dividing line lead people to conclude that there is not a real and important difference between taking good care and being negligent, or between being courageous and callous.

That's the way it should be. There is no clear point on the spectrum when red becomes orange or orange becomes yellow, but anyone who thought that meant there was no difference between red and yellow would need their logic as well as their eyes tested.

In the abortion debate, however, it is common to hear people point to the lack of a clear boundary between infant and fertilized cells as a reason to treat both identically. This is not a logical conclusion. All the lack of a clear boundary means is that we should err on the side of caution: it's better to make a car safer than is really essential than not quite safe enough; it's better to avoid anything that *might* cause an animal unnecessary distress than simply avoid those things we are sure will cause distress; and so on.

In practice, then, if we draw a line between acceptable abortion and *in utero* infanticide, it will be at a point that is in one sense arbitrary. But as long as it is arbitrary within a period of development when we are sure that the embryo is not deserving of the rights of a child, that arbitrariness is justified.

In deciding where to draw that line, biology becomes as important as philosophy. From philosophy we need to know the morally significant characteristics that give a creature a right to life. From biology we need to know when those characteristics emerge. Among those who endorse abortion, most agree that for the first fourteen weeks the foetus is not sufficiently developed to be given the same protection as a child. Such judgements are based on facts about how much the foetus is aware of itself and the environment, how sensitive it is to pain, how far down the path it is to taking the form of its post-natal self and so on. There are various arguments for choosing various points in development as the significant ones, but it is sufficient for present purposes to understand the general case for accepting that there is such a point.

Of course, many maintain that no line can be drawn, not because the boundary between two morally different significant stages of development is blurred but because there is no such difference. Every human has the same right to life from conception. The two justifications for this position that we have so far looked at – the sanctity of life and the importance of mere species membership – do not appear up to the task. Are there any other arguments that are more powerful?

Many believe their religion demands an opposition to all abortion. Theologically speaking, however, it is not at all obvious that Christians or any other religious believers must oppose abortion. There is nothing in the Bible that is explicit on such matters, and evoking the sixth commandment simply begs the question, since the issue is whether or not abortion counts as murder. Other biblical passages cited are much vaguer. For instance, the Bible often talks about

God creating us in the womb, but since nobody doubts that we all start life in the womb, that doesn't seem to take us very far. Others might cite the famous passage in the Bible when Job says: 'the Lord gave, and the Lord hath taken away,'[33] but this doesn't clearly state that *only* God can take your life.

Some say that life is a gift from God and only God will take it away. One problem with that is, as the philosopher Mary Warnock put it, this sounds less like a gift than a loan. Some may accept this and say that is precisely what it is: our lives on earth are a kind of loan and we only get the gift of eternal life at the end of it if we do the right thing, which includes not taking life. But although that is coherent, there is simply no clear evidence that this is what the major religions really demand. And even if the general principle were clear, to apply it to the foetus from conception begs the question as to when life really begins. If there isn't a human being until at least fourteen days of foetal life, perhaps later, then the Lord has not yet given and there is nothing to be taken away.

Fuzzy life

It seems, then, that although many want to find clear lines between justified and unjustified killing, between a mere collection of cells and a human being worthy of the same rights as grown adults, no such clear line exists. This can be disturbing because, after all, this is a serious issue of life and death. We need as much clarity as possible when the stakes are so high. But if the world doesn't contain that degree of clarity then no amount of wishing that it does can change the fact. Sometimes we have to cope with uncertainty and vagueness even when dealing with the most profound and important issues of life. That, rather than any neat answer to the question of whether abortion is moral or not, is the clearest and most certain conclusion we can come to in this debate.

Should euthanasia be legal?
The right to end your own life

Imagine the thing you most fear, knowing it will happen, and being unable to do anything to prevent it, not because it is practically impossible, but because it is illegal. Imagine the person you love most in the world, suffering, wanting you to help remove the pain, and being unable to do so, again, not because you do not have the physical means, but because you lack the legal right.

I don't think I can imagine such things. It is as though my attempts at empathy generate such discomfort that, involuntarily, some kind of self-defence mechanism pulls the plug on my imagination. Brian Pretty didn't have to use his imagination: this was his reality. 'Diane had to go through the one thing she had foreseen and was afraid of – and there was nothing I could do to help,'[34] he said after his wife slipped into a coma after suffering breathing difficulties caused by motor neurone disease. Diane had fought a legal battle in the years before her death, trying to establish that her husband would not be prosecuted under the 1961 Suicide Act for aiding and abetting her suicide if she decided that her suffering became unbearable. She took her case to the United Kingdom's highest court, the House of Lords and also to the European Court of Human Rights. She lost, and in May 2002 she died in precisely the way she had been fighting to avoid.

So you can see why many people support 'the right to die'. The phrase is misleading, because it is not illegal (in most countries, at least) for an adult to commit suicide or to refuse life-saving treatment. But it is almost always illegal to help somebody else to die. And in order to take your own life painlessly, you often need such help, especially if you suffer from one of the terrible degenerative diseases of the nervous system, which can leave you dependent on others for even the most basic of human activities, such as eating, washing and going to the toilet.

People often have very strong intuitions on both sides of this debate. In order to think clearly about this most troubling of issues, we need to be very clear which question we are asking: whether assisted suicide is morally wrong or whether it should be legal. As we saw in the chapter *Are Drug Laws Morally Inconsistent?*, the two questions are related, but they are not the same, and the differences are critical.

The tragic imprecision of law

In the case of Diane Pretty, the Law Lords who passed judgment on her first appeal made it very clear that the UK law operates on the legal positivist assumption that the court is not 'entitled or fitted to act as a moral or ethical arbiter'. Its job is simply 'to ascertain and apply the law of the land as it is now understood to be'.[35] The key law in question was the European Convention on Human Rights, which was incorporated into UK law by the Human Rights Act 1998. Pretty's case hinged on the interpretation of article 2, which states 'Everyone's right to life shall be protected by law. No one shall be deprived of his life intentionally save in the execution of a sentence of a court following his conviction of a crime for which this penalty is provided by law.' Summing up Pretty's argument, Lord Bingham wrote that

> *the purpose of the article is to protect individuals from third parties (the state and public authorities). But the article recognizes that it is for the individual to choose whether or not to live and so protects the individual's right to self-determination in relation to issues of life and death.*

Her case also hinged on article 3 of the convention, which asserts 'No one shall be subjected to torture or to inhuman or degrading treatment or punishment.' Pretty's argument was that, deprived of the right to end her own life, she was in effect being subjected to inhuman suffering.

Pretty also pointed to article 8, which concerns respect for private and family life, and states that 'There shall be no interference by a public authority with the exercise of this right' except in specified cases where this is absolutely necessary. Finally, she cited article 14, which protects individuals against discrimination.

As the Law Lords made clear, in considering these claims, they were not asking themselves whether the law was *right* to prevent Pretty from getting help to take her own life, but only if the law *allowed* her to do so. They concluded it did not. The prohibition on assisted suicide did not, the judges ruled, contravene any of her rights set out in the European Convention on Human Rights. Those who thought the law wrong therefore have to try to change it, and several attempts have been made to do so, which at the time of writing have all been unsuccessful.

However, it does not necessarily follow that if a law has a consequence that is thought to go against what is right, that law must be changed. People say things like 'It shouldn't be allowed' and 'There should be a law against it' but often the reason why there isn't is that such laws would be impractical or have other bad effects. The tragedy of the law is that it must provide clear black and white rules when morality is full of shades of grey. To not accept this and to expect the law always to deliver the morally best outcome is unrealistic. Lord Bingham pointed out as much in his judgment when he quoted Dr Johnson as saying 'Laws are not made for particular cases but for men in general,' and 'To permit a law to be modified at discretion is to leave the community without law.'[36]

That is not to say that in their application of the law, the judges were acting as pure legal positivists, interpreting the law without regard to the moral purpose behind the European Convention of Human Rights. For instance, Lord Bingham explicitly referred to the risks of abuse, if the law were to be loosened up. He quoted a House of Lords select committee report which said

> *We are also concerned that vulnerable people – the elderly, lonely, sick or distressed – would feel pressure, whether real or imagined, to request early death. . . . we believe that the message which society sends to vulnerable and disadvantaged people should not, however obliquely, encourage them to seek death, but should assure them of our care and support in life.*

This is clearly a moral concern, and in referring to it Bingham effectively acknowledges that the court was not simply interpreting the law with no thought as to its moral content, but was taking into account its moral purpose.

The morality of assisted suicide

If we set aside the question of whether assisted suicide should be legal and simply consider its morality, what do we find? Pretty's case rested on four articles of the European Convention on Human Rights that have their basis in moral commitments. In the most general terms, these centred on the right of an individual to live autonomously and not be forced to do things against her will of interests, and the extremely high value placed on life. In debates over assisted suicide and abortion, it can seem as though different sides pick one of these values and throw out the rest, so they are either 'pro-life' or 'pro-choice'. But of course, almost everyone is pro-both. The disagreements arise when the two values clash and we have to decide which takes priority.

Sometimes that clash is rooted in a religious conviction. However, even for believers, religion does not settle the issues, because people from the same religions often disagree about the ethics of euthanasia and, despite the interpretations of some anti-abortion clerics, there is no clear prohibition against it in either the Hebrew or Christian Bibles.

The 'pro-life' stance is often (though not always) based on an idea of the sanctity of life, which we looked at in the previous chapter on abortion. Most people, if they were to be consistent, would accept that placing an extremely high value on life does not automatically mean that euthanasia is wrong. People like Diane Pretty do not take a dim view of life. Indeed, they might argue that they love life and that is precisely why they want to end it before it becomes intolerable. This may seem like a trivial example, but think of a serious artist who comes to believe that the quality of their work has been declining for several years. If they were to conclude that there is no way of reaching previous heights, they might retire rather than keep producing work that does not do justice to how it was at its best. Love and affection for the work is what leads her to cease it. The case of life itself is, of course, of a different order, but the principle is the same: if you have loved your life and know that all you can look forward to from now on is pain and suffering so intolerable that you cannot even take pleasure from those you most love, you might decide through love of life to end it.

Nonetheless, some do argue that life is of such value that it is always worth prolonging, no matter how horrible. But why would one think that? Does anyone seriously believe that it would be better if a person died at midday rather than was tortured for twelve hours from noon onwards and died at midnight? Surely everyone would prefer to die sooner than later in this situation. Although extreme, this example demonstrates the point that simply having more life does not mean having a better life overall. Quality matters as well as quantity.

Still, there are other arguments that use this very high, but not inviolable, value of life to oppose euthanasia. One is to argue that the stakes are so high that we should always err on the side of caution. You never know what might happen – a groundbreaking new scientific discovery, say – and just as long as there is a flicker of hope of some kind of further meaningful moment in life, even if there is no chance of a return to normality, then life should be preserved. A second, related argument is that if we start allowing assisted suicide in extreme cases, then we risk a slippery slope, where people will end their lives for much less serious reasons, perhaps under pressure from others, as Lord Bingham warned.

These two arguments are interesting because neither relies on the belief that assisted suicide is always wrong. Rather they both warn that allowing it is dangerous. In the first case, the danger is that in any given case we might be mistaken about how worthwhile the future life would be. In the second, the danger is that we might be opening the doors to more killing than we intended. These dangers, if real, should make us think very carefully about the legalization of euthanasia. It would be tragic if we made it legal because we thought it morally justified, but by doing so made matters worse by bringing about more unnecessarily premature deaths. However, it would still be important to remember that these are not reasons for thinking that assisted suicide is, in itself, always wrong.

I think it would also be wrong to see these objections as purely practical or legal rather than moral. The morality of

any action should not simply be seen as resting on its immediate effects, but on all its consequences, on other people, in
the long term and on one's own moral character. We surely
do need to take seriously the idea that an action may appear
right (or at least not wrong) in terms of its immediate effects
but that it might also be corrosive of certain values. This is
precisely how some people feel about aspects of consumer
culture. There seems to be nothing wrong with enjoying a
shopping trip or buying things to make you look good. But
when we do these things repeatedly, we risk becoming ever
more shallow, materialistic and focused on things that don't
matter. In a way which is in some senses similar and in
others very different, a society that permits assisted suicide
may, some would argue, come to value life less.

Risks have to be balanced, however, and we must ask
whether these risks of condoning euthanasia – legally or
morally – are graver than the harms caused by condemning
it. One argument on the pro-euthanasia side is that there is
manifest and avoidable suffering going on every day because
people cannot seek help to end their own lives. What is
more, when assisted suicide is illegal, some, anticipating
being helpless, may actually chose to end their lives earlier
than they would otherwise, while they are still capable of
doing it themselves. So while it may be important to point
to the dangers of allowing assisted suicide, their mere existence does not clinch the case.

Double effect

There is one more important consideration in this issue. In law and in morality, particularly in the Roman Catholic tradition, there is something known as the principle of double effect. This maintains that there is a difference between an action intended to cause death and one which can be foreseen to cause death, but is intended to cause something else. So, for example, a doctor may administer a high dose of morphine to a patient in the late stages of a terminal disease, intending to relieve pain, but knowing, as the patient does, that the dosage will kill her. This is not killing, because the death is a kind of 'side effect' the patient is willing to suffer. If, however, the doctor administers the drug with the sole intention of killing the patient, then that is an act of killing.

Is this a morally significant difference? Many are not convinced and believe that it simply provides a convenient smokescreen. In practice, this is surely often true. A doctor may intend to relieve pain but also to end the life, seeing that pain relief provides an opportunity to bring about the comfortable death the patient wants. Indeed, surely in some way, if death is not intended, then the doctor should not relieve the pain.

It is certainly the case that we do not think people are let off any responsibility for actions if their consequences are merely foreseen but not intended. If an army indiscrimi- nately bombs a civilian area for example, it is not good enough for them to say they only intended to kill the insur- gents active there and that the civilians were just an unfor- tunate side effect. We are morally obliged to consider all foreseeable consequences of our actions, not just those we intend.

So although there is clearly some difference between doing an action with the sole intention of ending a life and doing something else which has different or other inten- tions as well, this difference does not seem to be strong enough to, by itself, show that assisted suicide is wrong but that hastening death as a side effect of other treatment is not.

A clearer confusion

It would be odd to head this section 'conclusion' when we seem very far indeed from one. But, as I said in the preface, it is not my aim in this book to 'solve' all the big ethical dilemmas posed. Rather, it is to get us thinking more help- fully about them. We could very easily have simply consid- ered whether people have a moral right to assisted suicide and then simply slapped on the conclusion, 'therefore it should be legal' or 'therefore it should be illegal'. And this is indeed how many texts in moral philosophy present the debate. But I think it would be misleading to the point of irresponsibility to do this. If we are to think seriously about what the law should be on important moral issues, we have to be clear about the relationship between law and morality and why good laws can sometimes have tragic consequences. When they do, we should always ask if they could be better. It should not be assumed, for instance, that the only way to protect the vulnerable against feeling coerced into assisted suicide is to keep the law as it is. But laws almost always have to draw lines in ways that, from a moral point of view, either permit too much or too little.

When the European Court of Human Rights rejected her final appeal, Pretty said, 'The law has taken all my rights away.' We can understand why she thought that, but on reflection we can see that is far from the truth. The European Convention on Human Rights gave Pretty, and all EU citizens, a large number of very important rights. In Pretty's case, however, it did so at the price of denying her the rights that in her terrible but unusual case were most important. If there could be a way of enshrining all our rights in ways that don't involve such trade-offs, we should certainly do so. But we have to consider the possibility that this cannot be done and that, sometimes, laws that spring from good moral commitments can have some immoral consequences.

Is sex a moral issue?
Ethics beyond prudery

Sexual ethics seems such a quaint old subject. You won't find it discussed in many introductions to ethics. Peter Singer made only a cursory reference to it in his famous Practical Ethics, and only then to distinguish it from more serious ethical issues, saying, 'Sex raises no unique moral issues at all.'[37] Such has been the success of the almost complete purge of sex from the arena of serious ethical debate that when someone does raise the topic, we immediately suspect (often correctly) that that person has some conservative or religious axe to grind. That particular axe does not rear its head here, but nonetheless I think there are still some real, live issues in sexual ethics.

One reason why the sexual ethics can seem outdated is because, on the one hand, the old reasons for viewing sex as an ethical matter have been eroded whilst, on the other, better, different reasons for considering it a proper subject for ethics have not been acknowledged. If you had asked anyone 100 years ago why they should not have sex with whoever they wanted, the reasons would have seemed to be obvious. The practical consequences of an unwanted pregnancy or catching a venereal disease could be disastrous. Societies have a habit of erecting taboos around behaviour which harms the group and so the vast majority have sanctioned long-term monogamous pair bonds and condemned any other kind of sexual relationship. These norms were bolstered by theological claims along the lines that sex is a gift from God for use only within specially sanctioned relationships.

These religious, social and practical considerations no longer hold sway. Most people have ceased to believe the traditional tenets of the major faiths, while pregnancy and disease have both become less of a threat with the use of contraceptives, abortion, condoms, and, until AIDS, freely available treatment for the occasional slip-up. We may have been premature and complacent to think we can have risk-free sex, but a person can minimize these dangers with a few sensible precautions, such that they fall within acceptable limits. Most importantly for present purposes, these are all merely *practical* concerns, not *moral* ones. As long as you don't put others at risk of infection or unwanted pregnancy, it does not seem that these risks raise any more moral issues than mountain climbing or skydiving.

Not only do we appear to have no good reason not to indulge our lusts as much as opportunity, desire and our relationships allow, there also seems to be a positive incentive to do so. It has entered folk psychology that 'repression' is a bad thing, and expression of our sexuality is vitally important. So take away religion, take away the fear of disease and pregnancy, stir in some popular psychology and you end up with the question, 'Why not have as much sex as you can?' To this there seems no good objection.

Ethics and morality

But the short, somewhat crude, sketch of the transformation of popular thinking about sex is, to my mind, founded on a spurious view of ethics. We have become used to thinking about ethics in general, and sexual activity in particular, as a particular form of morality: namely a code of conduct setting out behaviour which is or is not acceptable, desirable or required. There are rules which we ought to live by and breaking the rules is, well, immoral.

The problem here is that for such a moral system to have any force, there must be both a respected source for the code and a set of sanctions to ensure it is followed. In the language of the law, that means we need a legislator and an empowered judiciary. When religion was seen as the source of morality, this was no problem. God was both law-giver and law-enforcer (even though he usually postponed punishment until the afterlife). Now when we are at the stage when even many of those who believe in a god do not see either the church or any of the sacred texts as reliable sources, there is no longer any acknowledged moral legislature.

So have we reached the end of morality? If by morality we mean that kind of authority-rooted rule system described above (which is how I shall use the word from now on), then we quite possibly have. But although ethics-as-morality is almost certainly the most commonly held view of ethics in society in general, it is not the only one. In fact, the major alternative is older than even morality. Pick up a treatise on ethics by one of the great ancient Greeks and you'll be struck by how little 'morality' in the above sense they contain. What they are repeatedly concerned with is what is required to live the good life. But the 'good' of the ancients is not the 'good' of morality, as Nietzsche most famously observed.[38] 'Good' for the ancient Greeks stands in opposition to 'bad'. What is good is what makes a life go well. Friends, health, honour and integrity all go into making a life go well and so are considered good. Poverty, isolation and disenfranchise-ment all help a life go badly and so are bad. The poor person is not bad in the moral sense of the word, but it is almost always the case that the poor person is living a life which is going badly in significant ways. If we did not think this we would not feel under any moral obligation to help alleviate poverty. So what happens when we start to think about sexual ethics, not in terms of moral rules and prohibitions, but in terms of the role of sex in a life going well?

Sex and the good life

There are two alternative ways of trying to make your life go better. One way is to approach each situation with a calculating eye, weigh up what the pros and cons of each situation are and go for the most advantageous. This would seem to foster a sexual opportunism. For example, a woman is on holiday, away from her long-term partner. She meets an attractive man and the opportunity for a casual encounter arises. What is she to do? If she goes to bed with the man, there are obvious advantages for her and the man. Given that her partner will never know about this, there is no harm to him. Indeed, depending on the personalities involved, it may be good for the relationship. Coming back from her holiday rejuvenated helps them both; coming back resentful at having missed an opportunity thanks to her feelings of obligation to her partner may breed only resentment. Doing her ethical sums, the woman concludes that life goes better for everyone if she has her fling.

Of course, this is not the only way to tell the story. If the woman will feel guilty, if the man turns out to be a psychopath, if she cannot guarantee secrecy, the calculations are changed. But the calculations do often work out as I have described them. In fact, I would wager that this type of reasoning is precisely what allows millions of people worldwide to justify their unfaithfulness every year.

What this reveals is that, perhaps without it being explicitly recognized, consequentialism has established itself as
the implicit ethic of our time. It comes in a socially responsible form – 'if it doesn't harm anyone, there's nothing
wrong with it' – and an egotistical one – 'if I can get away
with it, I'll do it'. Both forms share two vital features. First,
they are not moral in the old sense of the word. They are not
concerned with following rules, but assessing individual
actions or sets of actions on their own merits. Secondly,
they both implicitly embrace the view of ethics as being
about 'life going well'. In the first version, all lives are
considered, in the latter, only the life of the agent herself.

The persuasiveness of this ethic is demonstrated by how
frequently a person will defend doing something generally
considered wrong by saying, 'It's not harming anyone.'
That is why sexual promiscuity has ceased to be taboo: a
very large number of people just don't believe that it causes
any harm.

There is, however, a second, alternative view of how one
can make one's life go better, one based on character, or in
the old-fashioned term, virtue. Let us return to the holi-
daying woman. The calculations seem straightforward. But
hang on a minute. If this is the way she runs her life, what is
the relationship with her partner really going to be like? Let
us assume they know each other well enough to know how
they think ethically. He knows that she will always do what's

good for her if it won't harm him, even if that involves lying, unfaithfulness and deceit. Would that affect the relationship? This realization may undermine one of the core pillars of a relationship – trust. He cannot trust her because there is nothing she would not do if the pay-off was good enough. And if he cannot rely on her faithfulness, why should he be faithful? Even if the opportunity never arises for his partner, in the same situation himself, he would know that she would go ahead. So why not him?

Now there are some couples for whom it is enough to know that their partner wouldn't harm them, and who are either perfectly happy not to be told about affairs or to hear about them. But I think such couples are extremely rare. For these people, there is nothing on this character or virtue view of ethics which would suggest their behaviour is wrong. Unless one believes that human nature is absolutely uniform, we cannot escape the conclusion that what is good for one person may not always be good for another. This is not a pernicious form of relativism because the same principle of 'a life going well' is being applied to all people. We are simply acknowledging that not all people are the same, and so what can help one person's life go well may not help another. Giving paints to an artist helps her life go well; giving them to an athlete is no good at all.

All my example shows is that taking each case as it comes *can* undermine the features of character which are important for a life to really go well in the long run. Intimate, trusting and close relationships are considered by the vast majority of people and experts in psychology to be a good thing, something which can really make a difference to the quality of life. But we cannot enjoy these relationships unless we have the character traits of integrity, loyalty and steadfastness. Opportunism and a calculating nature erode our capacity for them.

Aristotle was smart enough to realize that characters need to be formed and reinforced by custom and habit if they are to really stick. We cannot choose to switch character traits on and off at will. That is why the way in which we conduct our sex lives before, between or after committed relationships is also important. Promiscuity can foster several character traits which arguably do not help the individual in the long run. Individuals do, of course, differ, so what follows is not necessarily true for all people. But enough of it is true for enough people for it to merit serious consideration.

First, promiscuity fosters opportunism, the tendency to go for what appears to be of immediate benefit. This is certainly not helpful, and sometimes disastrous, when the person is involved in a long-term relationship. This point could be supported by game theory, but common sense is just as good. People who can be trusted to behave honourably and consistently, without being pushovers, do better in the long run than those who actively seek their best advantage in each situation that comes along. The reason is simple: someone who is seen as an opportunist undermines trust in themselves, and without trust, we can't get the benefits of reciprocal exchange.

In a relationship, what that boils down to is that a loss of trust erects emotional barriers between you and your partner. Not only is it likely that we will be recognized as opportunists at the start of a relationship, which means creating trust is that much harder, for many it will be difficult to cease being opportunists, threatening the relationship in the future. We don't transform our personalities just because we've started a committed relationship.

Things get even worse when one adds the second set of personality traits promiscuity tends to encourage: guardedness and deceit. Again there are exceptions, but promiscuity generally involves hiding one's true feelings, motives, thoughts and desires from the people with whom we are most intimately involved. For someone who has nurtured these traits, it may actually be very hard to really start a committed relationship. If one is used to physical intimacy without emotional intimacy, it can be very hard to make the switch to openness which a really committed relationship requires.

The third trait is a tendency to objectify members of the opposite sex. It is not for nothing that certain pick-up joints are called 'meat markets'. When a person is basically looking for sex, and nothing else, almost inevitably people are viewed not as whole human beings, but for their sexual promise. Pornography has, for a long time, been criticized for treating women as objects, with all the wider consequences that entails. What is not so frequently noted is that promiscuity does a very similar thing to members of both sexes. If you were to eavesdrop on a group of men talking about a photo in a porn magazine and the same group talking about people they were eyeing up in a nightclub, you may not be able to tell which conversation was which. It seems one of the hollowest victories in the quest for gender equality that it is now equally acceptable for women to view men in the same way.

There are other traits that promiscuity often nurtures. One is cynicism. For all the hedonism promiscuity seems to involve, it is remarkable how it fails to make so many people happy about their private lives. To those for whom sex is just something you do with other people, and for whom everyone is just essentially out for their own good time, it is no wonder that ideas of love and commitment seem nothing more than fairy tales. How can you even believe in the promise of committed, emotional relationships when your encounters reinforce time and again the message that people are just out for what they can get?

Finally, and perhaps most controversially, although there is something flattering about being desired by a member of the opposite sex, in the long run, I doubt promiscuity generally helps one's self-esteem. In being promiscuous we treat others and are treated as nothing more than a means to the end of sexual gratification. But surely we all want to be valued as more than just that. We need to be accepted as whole persons, not just as instruments of pleasure.

The return of ethics

I may not be right about all of the above, and I have certainly not considered any of the positive traits which promiscuity may help to instil (although other than helping one stay in touch with one's desires, I'm not sure how many I could come up with). But even if I am half-right, I will have done enough to establish that sex does entail some important ethical considerations. The result is not a prude's charter. A rejection of promiscuity – even if that is what my argument entails – does not require a retreat to celibacy or a one partner, one life policy. What I am more concerned with doing is establishing that there is a serious way of looking at sexual ethics which has nothing to do with old-fashioned moralizing and which offers more than a crude appeal to best consequences. For our lives to go well, most of us need to build the types of character which enable us to engage in honest and committed relationships. There are many reasons for believing that sexual opportunism undermines some of those character traits. So we should consider what type of attitude to sex develops the most beneficial character traits. This does lead us to 'shoulds', but not the finger-wagging ones of the old sexual morality. They are conditional: if we want our lives to go as well as they can, then we should try and think a bit more about the implications of how we conduct our sex lives.

This is a conclusion that will certainly be too weak for the old-fashioned moralists. It doesn't rule out all one-night stands. It doesn't rule out partner-swapping for those who can honestly live with all that entails. There may even be a significant number of people who really do suit a life of free love. But it does provide us with a framework within which we can start to seriously think about sexual ethics again. If we acknowledge the links that bind character, emotional relationships, our own well-being and the way we conduct our sex lives, it will not seem at all odd to think anew about the ethical implications of our private lives.

Can discrimination be good?
Sameness, difference and equality

Are you in favour of discrimination? Although the answer might seem obvious, it can vary considerably according to the context. To accuse someone of, say, racial discrimination is a serious charge. At the same time, it is hardly a term of praise to call someone an undiscriminating eater or appreciator of music. To discriminate simply means to make distinctions between things on the basis of a judgement of whether they are good or bad, better or worse. That's clearly unobjectionable when it comes to art or food. But is it ever justifiable to discriminate when it comes to people?

Two candidates are applying for a job. In terms of their aptitudes and suitability, both are equal except that the first has all the necessary experience and qualifications while the second does not. Is it justifiable to give the job to the first candidate?

Two students are applying for the last remaining place at a top university. One went to an elite private school and has top grades across the board. The other went to a state school in a deprived district and has very good grades, but only a few top ones. Is it justifiable to give the place to the state school student?

Two candidates, one male and one female, are applying for a job that requires the degree of physical strength that is much more common in men than women. Both are equally qualified. Is it justifiable to give the job to the man rather than the woman because he is a man?

A landlord is deciding whom to rent his apartment to. The letting agent offers a choice of two candidates. All the landlord knows is that one is a 30-year-old male tattoo artist, the other is a 40-year-old female academic. Is it justifiable for the landlord to choose the academic on the basis of this information alone?

A black American and a white American are applying for the same job and have the same qualifications. Is it justifiable to give the job to the white American because he is white?

Some libertarians would argue that if in each case the person or institution making the selection is a private one, then people are free to choose whoever they want, for good reasons or bad ones. In other words, some discrimination may be deplorable, but people are within their rights to practise it. If, however, by 'justifiable' we mean morally defensible, then few would answer yes to all five of these questions, and it is hard to see how they could do so unless they harboured unwarranted prejudices. Most would think that two of the answers are clear-cut, and the other three somewhat more difficult.

The easy dilemmas are the first and last. To choose a more qualified candidate over a less qualified one is to show discrimination of a sort, in that it shows an ability to distinguish between the qualities of different applicants. But this is perfectly acceptable and is not what we usually mean when we talk about discrimination in contexts such as hiring. The paradigm example of that kind of wrong discrimination is hiring a white person instead of a black one purely because he is white, as in the last example. The reason this is unacceptable is that it shows a lack of proper discrimination. The colour of one's skin is irrelevant to a person's abilities to do a job, and to make a decision about someone based on this factor is to show an ignorance of what the proper grounds of discrimination are – ability, aptitude, qualifications and so on.

We can instantly see, therefore, that the problem of discrimination is not whether to discriminate or not, but on what basis one discriminates. If you do so on the basis of factors that involve relevant differences between people, there is no problem. If you do so on the basis of irrelevant differences, then you're acting on the basis of ignorance or prejudice – which might perhaps be the same thing.

So what then should we say about the other three cases? Is it always clear where the difference between properly discriminating choices and prejudiced discrimination lies?

Group think

The obvious difference between the clearly acceptable and clearly unacceptable examples of discrimination given above was that the former distinguished between the people involved on the basis of their personal qualities (qualifications and experience), whereas the latter discriminated solely on the basis of group membership (skin colour). This might appear to offer a simple way of drawing the line between right and wrong forms of discrimination.

Take the example of the man and woman applying for a job that requires the degree of physical strength that is much more common in men than women. Although it may be true that each belongs to a group that, on average, has different levels of physical strength, that difference by itself provides no justification for choosing the man over the woman. The reason for this is simple: the characteristics of the group are mere averages, and any given woman may be stronger than any given man. Since the requirement of the job is strength, not gender, the employer can and should simply design the selection process to test the strength of the candidates and judge them accordingly. If the candidates are in all other respects equal but the woman is stronger, she should get the job. There is no good reason to judge her, as an individual, according to the average characteristics of her sex.

This is an important point. In order to justify differential hiring and recruiting policies, people often point to research purportedly showing real differences between men's and women's aptitudes and abilities. But as John Stuart Mill argued in 1869, if these differences are so strong that no woman can do a 'man's job', discrimination is unnecessary: 'What women by nature cannot do, it is quite superfluous to forbid them from doing. What they can do, but not so well as the men who are their competitors, competition suffices to exclude them.'[39] So if the differences are mere averages, any given individual woman may well be up to the task and allowed the opportunity to prove herself. (And the same is obviously true of men who are thought incapable of doing 'women's work'.)

But what if you are not in a position to assess the merits of each individual? Would it then be justifiable to use the typical characteristics of the group as the best available evidence to make a decision? If, for example, you have to. choose an applicant on the basis of written applications only and you have no data on physical strength, would you be justified in giving the job to the man on the basis that he is more likely to be physically stronger?

This is similar to the choice presented to the landlord who wants her tenant to be clean and tidy. Obviously she does not and cannot know just how fastidious her potential tenants are. But she does believe that younger male tattoo artists are in general less clean than older female academics. If this is so, then isn't she justified in preferring the older woman?

There are several questions that need to be considered before we can decide how to answer. The first is whether or not the supposed differences between typical behaviours of each group are in fact real. There is plenty of empirical evidence that women, on the whole, keep their homes cleaner than men. This does not necessarily mean that they are naturally more domestic than men, of course: the difference could be a product of social conditioning. But the difference is there. On the other hand, does the landlord have any evidence to believe that tattoo artists are less fastidious than academics? Probably not. That would appear to be a prejudice. Indeed, given that tattoo artists need to keep their equipment and studios clean, while academics are notoriously prone to allow their offices to pile up with used coffee cups and papers, it might even turn out that tattoo artists make for better tenants than professors.

So, even if it is true that, on average, women keep cleaner and tidier homes than men, you still have to ask, given what else we know about the prospective tenants, whether or not overall we have any reason to expect one to be better house-keepers than the other. In this case, the answer is probably no. Gender is a poor predictor of whether any given individual will be clean and tidy, as is a person's profession, on which the evidence is equally unclear. What's more, in the case we have just looked at, the mere fact that both potential tenants are interested in the same flat suggests that they share similar values about what a desirable home is.

We now have two reasons why it might be wrong to discriminate on the basis of group membership. First, it is wrong to judge a person on the basis of group averages when we can judge them on their own merits. Second, even when we cannot judge them on their own merits, it is wrong to use group membership as a criterion when it does not give a reliable enough indicator of the likely behaviour of the individual.

But what if the average differences between groups is significant and there is no way to judge on individual merits? This would be the case of the male and female applicants for whom physical strength mattered but could not be assessed. Is it reasonable to use group membership as the basis of discrimination here?

In general, we do accept that it is rational to use clear differences in averages as the basis for choices, even when we know they do not reliably predict what will actually be the case. For example, it is rational to choose to visit a country during a month that is on average warmer and drier than another, even when there is a significant possibility that it will actually be cool and damp after all. Similarly, it is rational to order a product from a company whose service you have previously found to be better than another, even though it is possible the alternative has improved or might be better in this particular case. What other basis can we use but probability to make choices when we cannot know for sure what the outcome will be? If this is true in the case of holidays and washing machines, why can't it also be true in the case of tenants and employees?

One answer is that it is very important we do not entrench the kinds of prejudices that favour one group over another. So, even if it is true that, on average, some groups perform tasks better than others, we still should not discriminate on the basis of group membership because we should not reinforce habits that lead individuals to be judged according to stereotypes. The force of this argument depends, I think, on how significant the group differences really are. In the real world, there are very few jobs where simply knowing whether a candidate is, say, male or female tells you more about their suitability for a job than their experience, qualifications and motivation. So, using sex would be to give too much weight to what is, in the bigger picture, not a very significant factor. On the other hand, it is not difficult to think of some cases where ignoring average group differences would appear to be absurd. Choosing someone very small and light over someone tall and sturdy for a job that requires heavy lifting, for instance, would appear to be perverse. However, the truth is that in the real world such cases are rare. In almost every case, either we can assess people as individuals or the group differences are not strong enough to justify using them as the basis for discrimination. That, and the desirability of perpetuating an ethos in which people are not judged on the basis of group membership, would be enough to suggest that in almost all – but not quite perhaps literally all – cases, it is wrong to discriminate on the basis of group difference, even when those differences are real.

Correcting for injustice

But is there an important exception to this rule? Take the example of the two students applying to a top university, one from an elite private school and one from a state school in a deprived district. There are very good reasons for thinking that people get better grades if they go to better schools. That is, after all, one of the main reasons why parents are prepared to spend so much money sending their children to good schools. This generally means that a student who does well at a poor school would almost certainly do better at an excellent one. If this is so, why not factor this in when assessing the merits of the students? If a university wants to attract the best students surely it should make sure that it is not missing out on great talents whose abilities are not accurately reflected in their grades?

I think this is a compelling argument. Many do not accept it on the basis that it unfairly discriminates against privately educated children as a group, not on their individual merits. But this is not the same kind of situation as simply using average group characteristics as a criterion. Rather, it is using established facts about the effects of social background to assess individuals in certain groups more accurately than relying on exam results alone. Facts about the group are therefore being used to make the individual assessment more accurate, not to replace an individual assessment.

This is also different from some other forms of 'positive discrimination'. For example, sometimes organizations decide they will hire more women, because although there appear to be no reasons why men are more suited to the work then women, there are many more men employed than women, and so they suspect there is some kind of prejudice that needs correcting. How they set about doing this, however, can vary enormously. The closest parallel to the state student case would be if the organization tried to identify why it was women were losing out to men who were no more or perhaps less able than them. There may have been a systematic bias built into the selection procedure, or interviewers may have been unaware of their own unconscious prejudices, or perhaps advertisements were inadvertently putting women off applying. By making changes and perhaps factoring in some information, the employer might treat female applicants differently so as to ensure that they are not overlooked. Still, the goal would be to assess each candidate on his or her merits.

But another option is simply to introduce a quota and try to employ more women, even if there is no good reason to think that the chosen female candidates are better than the rejected male ones. This is a form of positive discrimination that is based on facts about a group as a whole and not the individual. Is this ever justifiable? Many believe it is not. Even if it is true that women are discriminated against in the workplace, two wrongs do not make a right. If it is wrong to employ a man because he is a man, it is also wrong to employ a woman because she is a woman. If there is an equality problem, the answer lies not with positive discrimination but affirmative action: taking steps to encourage the disadvantaged group to compete on their merits, by such means as deliberately encouraging them to apply, making it easier for them to attend interviews, and so on.

Personally, I think the case for affirmative action is stronger than that for positive discrimination. But there is at least one reason why we should nonetheless at least consider positive discrimination in some circumstances. The fact is, as psychologists, sociologists and anthropologists well understand, prejudices can be very deeply entrenched and cannot simply be overridden by a well-intentioned desire to treat everyone equally – if we try to correct social injustice by relying on people making fair decisions, without prejudice, we are probably not going to fully succeed. In that case, isn't there an argument that we need to force the hands of recruiters and employers? By saying you must employ a certain proportion of women, ethnic minorities, people with disabilities and so forth, we might overcome prejudice more effectively than by appealing to values of fairness alone. Although on paper this ruling seems to be unfair, it may sometimes be the only means of overcoming the inevitable unfairness that results when people are left to decide for themselves.

Discriminating judgements

Having discussed a number of scenarios what should be clear is that different circumstances call for very different responses. There is no one simple thing called 'discrimination' which is just or unjust. There are many forms of discrimination and many reasons for discriminating, some good and some bad, all depending on the particular situation. The best reason for avoiding pernicious forms of discrimination is that it is unjust to make sweeping generalizations that do not account for the merits of each individual person. It would be ironic if, in supporting this noble aim, opponents of discrimination themselves ended up making sweeping generalizations that do not account for the merits of each individual case.

Is free trade fair trade?
The ethics of global business

Around the start of the second decade of the 21st century, a few years after the biggest global recession since the 1930s, Western economies were either teetering along or threatening to slide back into recession. Talk of the failures of the market were not confined to the left-wing fringes but were common among mainstream economists and conservative politicians. The question of whether a market economy can both work and work fairly has moved from the fringes to the heart of political debate.

'Market failure' can mean two things: a moral failure to deliver a just distribution of wealth or a practical failure to function efficiently. The two kinds of failure may be related, but they are quite distinct, and it can look like wishful thinking when those who have moral objections to capitalism are quick to claim that it is actually unsustainable.

The key feature of a completely free market is that there are no controls on what anyone pays for anything, including labour. Prices are set by supply and demand. If people want or need something, they will pay for it. But if you try to charge too much, they simply won't buy, and so you will be forced to bring your prices down. If you charge too little, on the other hand, people will snap it up and you'll be left with nothing to sell, so you will naturally raise your prices. If people want a lot of something and it is possible to produce more of it, then production will increase as the opportunity to make money is recognized. If people want a lot of something and it isn't possible to increase production, it becomes very expensive.

Crucially, it is argued that this is not just efficient but fair. There is no 'natural' cost of a product or commodity that could be worked out in any other way. Think, for example, of the price of potatoes compared to caviar. Is one more expensive than the other because it is inherently tastier? I don't think so. I'd wager that if potatoes were rare they'd be the most sought after, expensive foodstuff in the world. Chips are delicious, but because they're plentiful they're cheap. Caviar is quite nice, but because it's rare its flavour is more novel and people are prepared to pay more to eat it less often. (They may often be prepared to pay just because it is expensive, of course, but that's another matter.)

You might think that the price set by the market cannot be fair for two reasons. First of all, some things are more essential than others and it cannot be right that, if they are scarce, then the poor can't afford them. Take the market rate for retroviral drugs to combat HIV and Aids, for example. The market price of this is too high for people in the developing world to afford, and so it cannot be fair. The second reason is that people can abuse a monopoly to charge as much as they like for things people really need. If I charge too much for a designer handbag and some people are silly enough to pay anyway, so be it. But if I charge too much for a vital medicine or clean water, people will just have to pay, and I can get rich off their need. Although in theory others could come and compete with me, driving down prices, in practice that can't always happen. In a sparsely populated area, or closed environments like airports, for example, people have no option to go elsewhere. It also takes time for rivals to start up and costs may be prohibitive.

There are, however, standard answers to this. In a truly fair market, monopolies will be rare. Where prices are made artificially high, it is usually because of price-fixing by cartels or misplaced regulation preventing competitors setting up. It is true that free markets therefore need policing – they cannot be completely unregulated or else cartels will exploit consumers. But they need policing in order to be truly free, not because their freedom is the problem.

There may still be cases when the prices of essentials still remain too high for the poor. But such situations do not necessarily show that the system is in general flawed. It might simply mean that in some instances, as a society we might want to subsidize certain essentials in the name of social justice. In other words, we might think the free market has limits which we need to work around, rather than that it just doesn't work and we must abandon it. The former is actually the way in which Western liberal democracies work: they allow free markets most of the time but also intervene to lower the costs of things like medicines and public transport.

Some defenders of the free market think this already concedes too much. The problem is, they argue, that people assume that inequality is a sure sign of injustice, whereas actually it's just a sign that people are free to live their own lives and so have different outcomes. In fact, some argue that what looks like injustice is often entirely justified.

Defending the free market

Take just one example of an apparent injustice in global capitalism. Around the world, there are people working long hours for little pay, in sometimes dangerous, dirty or just unpleasant conditions. Whether they are growing cheap crops or stitching expensive designer clothes, only a tiny fraction of what we pay goes back to them. How can that be fair?

One answer is that they are not slaves: no one is forcing them to take the work. They do it of their own free will because they judge it is better than the alternatives. As Johan

Norberg, author of *In Defence of Global Capitalism*, put it, 'In a typical developing nation, if you're able to work for an American multinational, you make eight times the average wage. That's why people are lining up to get these jobs.'[40]

The key concept here is 'informed consent'. If someone is tricked into prostitution, or told they are going to be paid well and actually given a pittance, that's one thing. But if they take on a job in the full knowledge of what they are getting into, no matter how dangerous or unpleasant it is, shouldn't we just assume they are making a rational choice for themselves and not agonize over their plight?

It's a reassuring argument, since if it works, our consciences can be cleared. But the idea that there is no problem as long as there is consent is flawed for several reasons.

First, people sometimes have to choose terrible things because in practical terms they have no choice. Prostitution is a good example. I'm sure there are some women for whom sex work is not a last resort but a deliberate career move, but in many cases they are driven to it out of desperation. Any man who thinks prostitution is never exploitative just as long as the woman isn't being physically forced into the job is surely deluded.

Second, the fact that something unpleasant is the best choice available to someone doesn't make it OK, if we could be offering them a better one at little or no cost. It is not uncommon for managers in factories in the developing world that supply the West to refuse their workers sufficient toilet breaks, deny them drinking water, fail to follow local laws or health and safety procedures – the list could go on. So what if working in one of these places is still the best option locally? If paying a little bit more could remove all these hardships, why not do it? People may be queuing up to take these jobs, as Johan Norberg claims, but people queue up for all sorts of things when they're in dire need. He also throws in a red herring when he says 'If workers were paid US wages in Vietnam, employers wouldn't be able to hire them.' The choice is not between sweatshops or Western pay and conditions, it's between the opportunity to earn a decent living in a decent job, and working long hours in poor conditions for barely enough to live on.

For it to genuinely be the case that making a choice means it is no one else's business what happens to you, the choice has to be genuinely informed, a real rather than a forced one, and what people do to you subsequently still has to be as fair as can be reasonably expected of them. Can we honestly say these conditions are met for people who work in sweatshops? I don't think so.

A second, related argument is that this kind of work is better than nothing. For example, the National Center for Policy Analysis (NCPA), whose goal it is 'to develop and promote private alternatives to government regulation and control, solving problems by relying on the strength of the competitive, entrepreneurial private sector', has argued that,

> *Although conditions in many of the [sweat]shops are admittedly wretched, people chose to work in the shops of their own free will, experts point out, because a lousy job is better than none at all.*[41]

So it's not just that workers choose these jobs freely, but that if we don't buy goods which come from sweatshops, the workers we are concerned about will be worse off, since their poorly paid, tough and often dangerous jobs are better than no jobs at all, or the alternatives open to them.

The argument has a good pedigree. Lucy Martinez-Mont's *Wall Street Journal* article 'Sweatshops Are Better than No Shops' is a much-cited example. In it she wrote,

> *Banning imports of child-made goods would eliminate jobs, hike labour costs, drive plants from poor countries and increase debt. Rich countries would sabotage Third World countries and deny poor children any hope of a better future.*[42]

What Martinez-Mont says is true. But it doesn't follow that we can therefore carry on buying child-produced goods with impunity, because the choice is not between the status quo and banning such imports. This is something most 'fair trade' campaigners know full well. For example, the Maquila Solidarity Network advised, 'Don't promote a blanket boycott of all goods produced by child labour,' precisely on the grounds that simply withdrawing custom and leaving nothing in its place is harmful to those they want to help. The Ethical Trade Initiative base code prohibits 'new recruitment of child labour', and insists that member companies

shall develop or participate in and contribute to policies and programmes which provide for the transition of any child found to be performing child labour to enable her or him to attend and remain in quality education until no longer a child.

The point is simple. Poor working conditions may be better than nothing, but that does not justify us supporting such conditions. The alternative should not be nothing, but making things better. Parents who feed their child junk food cannot say that they should not be criticized because junk food is better than no food, because there is the option of offering proper food. Likewise, there are now many alternatives we all have to buying products which rely on exploited labour, if we can be bothered to make a little effort to ask questions about suppliers.

The core of the free market defence, however, is a factual claim that the developing world needs a genuinely free global market, not the good-intentioned indulgence of liberals. Coffee farmers would have no trouble making a good living from their beans if advanced Western nations eliminated import tariffs, farm subsidies and other distortions to the market.

The main problem with this argument is that it is premised on the fact that there isn't at present the kind of free market that there should be. But it is very difficult to know whether a genuinely free market would deliver the kind of fairness promised, although to this non-economist it does look unlikely.

From a practical point of view, however, the real question is not what would happen if global trade were truly free, but what we can do as things are now. Maybe farmers in the developing world would be better off if borders were open. But they are not. So, in the real world, the question is how should we act faced with the choice between buying goods in a distorted market that squeezes suppliers and buying goods that don't contribute to this squeezing. And the only ethically acceptable answer is that we should not squeeze suppliers as hard as we can.

But what about our choices as individuals in the status quo? I have suggested that we should try to buy products that are 'fairly traded'. But some economists object to this, saying that it distorts markets and ultimately causes more harm than good. For instance, the free market think tank the Adam Smith Institute claimed,

By paying higher than market prices, [Fairtrade] ensures that its favoured farmers do not have to respect market conditions which might tell others to cut back production in the event of a world surplus. They continue to plant and expand production, adding to the surplus and depressing prices for millions of poor farmers.

This is also the case made by Peter Griffiths in *Prospect* magazine, in which he insisted that this is a profoundly moral point. 'This is not just a matter of one lot of farmers receiving a little more and another lot a little less,' he wrote.

It means subsidizing 1.5m coffee workers while paying 25m farm families – the coffee growers who are not part of Fairtrade – a lot less. Most of these are subsistence producers, whose income from coffee is tiny. Any fall in income will mean children dying from malnutrition or malaria.

I'm no economist, but I struggle to see the logic in this position. The argument rests on the case that Fairtrade farmers being paid more than the market value sends some kind of signal to other producers, or drives down their prices. But those outside the Fairtrade scheme take their cues from what is happening in the non-Fairtrade market. In any case, Fairtrade is a small proportion of the world market. It is not yet able to have such wide ripple effects on the wider economy, as did Cambodia's disastrous attempt to become the world's leading coffee producer.

Director of the Fairtrade Foundation Harriet Lamb rejects Griffith's argument, countering that Fairtrade coffee growers are small-scale or subsistence farmers just like most growers. The big difference is that they can sell some of their crops at a minimum price to cover the cost of production and help pay for business or community improvements. She explains,

> *Rather than encouraging the planting of more coffee, this brings the opportunity to improve quality and diversify into other income sources. So if the Fairtrade market expands, more farmers will have a better chance to work their way out of poverty, rather than relying on charity.*

But the reason I'm most baffled by free-market-based objections to Fairtrade is that such initiatives are free market mechanisms *par excellence*. How does a free market work? On the basis of supply and demand. Prices are not fixed by governments or regulators but set by market conditions. If a product becomes plentiful and demand is constant, prices fall. If demand increases but production does not, prices rise.

In such a market, no prices are what is usually called 'artificially high'. It is because Fairtrade coffee (to stick to that example) appears to have an artificially high price that it rings alarm bells with many economists. However, this is not a market-bucking premium but a market-dependent one. The price is higher solely because consumers want to pay the extra for the benefits they believe that produces. In this sense, the fair trade premium is no different from any other premium that consumers in a free market choose to pay. Indeed, it is smaller and less spurious than many others. For example, people are willing to pay extra for a celebrity-endorsed product, or one with a logo. The power of brands is largely the fact that they enable producers to get people to pay more than they otherwise would. Yet I do not hear economists protesting that Adidas T-shirts are artificially expensive and so distort markets.

Free and fair?

Free trade can be fair. Normally speaking, if I have something you want, then I should not be forced to part with it for less than I am willing to. We should be free to make and sell what we want. However, there are certain inequalities and asymmetries in trading relationships that can make them unfair. One such case is when I exploit a monopoly or collude in a cartel to keep prices artificially high. Another, which we looked at in the chapter *How Much Should We Give to Charity?* is where I maximize my profits by employing low-paid workers and providing only poor conditions, when I could easily do better without significant cost to myself.

It therefore seems to be the case that we do not need to dismantle the broadly free-trade-based system we have to achieve more social justice. All we need do – which is actually quite a lot – is to regulate in order to limit the harmful effects of free markets by insisting on minimum standards for workers at the end of supply chains, and to intervene to ensure that essential goods that the poor cannot afford are made available to them if at all possible. It's not as exciting as a revolution, perhaps. But sometimes another world is possible by making a few changes to the one we have, rather than by replacing it with something completely different.

Should we protect the environment?

On whether nature can be harmed

Most of the controversy around anthropogenic (human-made) climate change concerns if, and how quickly, it is happening. Although the vast majority of the scientific establishment agrees that it is, a significant minority, who cannot all be dismissed as apologists for big polluters and carbon-based fuel extractors, continues to insist that the threats have been exaggerated.

This debate, however, is essentially a purely factual and pragmatic one about whether or not climate change is happening, whether its effects will, on balance, be bad, and whether we can do anything to stop the damage happening or at least minimize it. The moral issues are not insignificant: they include who picks up the tab for the remedial work, the rich or the poor, this generation or those to come. Nevertheless, they are not the core ones.

There is, however, another dimension to the environmental debate, one that gets mixed up with the practical, factual one, often with the effect of not so much muddying the waters as turning an already heavily silted river to sludge.

This is the question of whether there is something immoral about damaging the environment, regardless of the consequences for us. Many talk as though it were. People use phrases like the 'rape of the earth', the 'plundering of the planet', the 'despoiling of nature' and so on.[43] It is not just that what humanity is doing threatens its own survival, the victim of these crimes is nature herself, Gaia.

Whether or not we accept that it is morally wrong to harm nature makes a big difference to how we respond to global warming and other environmental threats. So how do we make sense of this? We can start by asking: just what is nature?

The invention of nature

One of the most important events in human history was the discovery – or perhaps invention – of nature in the sixth century BC. Almost everything we take for granted in the modern world owes its origins to that breakthrough in human thought.

Before a group of Ionian philosophers known as the Milesians, there was no distinction between the natural and the supernatural. If you wanted to know why it rained, the gods' intentions were as pertinent, if not more so, as the movements of the clouds. Hence in Deuteronomy, God promised to 'give you the rain of your land in his due season' if his commands were followed or to 'shut up the heaven, that there be no rain, and that the land yield not her fruit' if they were not.[44] In Homer, a goddess, Circe, 'sent a favouring wind that filled the sails, a kindly escort'.[45] In such a world, nature had yet to be given a life of its own, for it was one with the supernatural.

What the Milesians realized was that it was possible to explain what goes on in nature without recourse to the desires and intentions of any supernatural entities. Whereas the will of the gods remained mysterious, nature was scrutable. Humanity could understand it and, to a certain extent, master it. This conceptual breakthrough made science and philosophy possible.

This intimate connection between a proper understanding of what nature is and the very possibility of true knowledge of how the world works completely inverts the modern myth that nature contrasts or conflicts with science and technology. We think of nature romantically as the world untouched by humanity, a given which we can use wisely or abuse foolishly. Such a view separates nature from human understanding when the truth is that we only came to know what nature was when we realized it was a fit and proper object of human knowledge. We should not then talk wistfully of primitive societies living in harmony with nature but in ignorance of it.

This is why complaints that any time we 'tamper' with nature we are hubristically 'playing God' are so misplaced. The French mathematician and astronomer LaPlace told

Napoleon he had no need of the hypothesis of God in his cosmology, but the same could be said of any scientific account. We do not play God when we manipulate nature because nature is controlled by impersonal forces, not a deity. Even religious scientists who believe that God created the universe and established scientific laws do not usually believe that he is pulling the strings from moment to moment. Only by blurring the natural/supernatural distinction can the claim that science interferes with divine will make sense.

It might be thought that this genealogy of the concept of nature is irrelevant to the concerns of those who are worried about the human relationship to the natural world today. Surely we all know what Prince Charles meant when, in accepting the Grande Médaille of the French Société de Géographie, he said, 'if we fail to understand that true sustainability depends on accepting certain limits to human ambition and working more in harmony with the mysterious processes of Nature, then we face a social and natural catastrophe of unimaginable proportions'.[46] The message seems clear: we work in harmony with nature when we seek to change it as little as possible and not 'interfere' with the 'the mysterious processes of Nature'. But this prescription does not stand up to scrutiny.

The idea that we should interfere with the world as little as possible is vacuous. Every human advance that has ever taken place has involved altering the world, whether it was by building artificial shelters, farming rather than gathering, or just starting fires. The huge decrease in the number of women who die in childbirth and children who perish because of poor sanitation, or the much-increased lifespan of people in the Western world, all depend upon humanity making the world different to how we found it. Given how much we have already altered the world in which we live, to say that at a certain point further such alterations work against the grain of nature whereas previous ones did not looks not only Canute-like but conceptually incoherent.

What of the idea that working with nature means going along with its powers and not resisting them? Such notions explain the preference many have for 'natural remedies' over modern pharmaceuticals. The reasoning seems to be that natural treatments simply harness nature's latent powers whereas modern drugs seek to usurp them.

But the distinction simply doesn't work. If a medicine works it is precisely because it is harnessing a power in nature to heal. No pharmaceutical can work by trying to defy natural laws. All medicine is an attempt to pit one causal power over another, to fight that part of nature that harms us with another part which heals us. As the physicist Richard Feynman observed, 'For a successful technology, reality must take precedence over public relations, for Nature cannot be fooled.'[47]

In the same way, every scientific advance has to work with the grain of nature because science does not defy natural laws: it is constrained by them. It is not science that dispenses with nature, but many of the alternative forms of medicine and explanation, which are premised on the existence of supernatural forces. Indeed, in invoking 'the mysterious processes of Nature', Prince Charles seemed to be harking back to the world view of Homer, for whom nature truly was mysterious because it was controlled by fickle gods, not predictable, impersonal laws.

It is nonetheless true that many of the problems that it is claimed the world faces as nature becomes more and more under our control are real. There are serious issues of pollution, global warming and biotechnology. These problems are not illusory. How then can a proper understanding of what nature is help us to address these genuine dilemmas?

Only by properly understanding what nature is can we avoid red herrings and ensure we focus on what the real problems are. Take global warming, for example. In its last report, the International Panel on Climate Change, the most authoritative source of scientific information on this phenomenon, concluded that 'During the past 50 years, the sum of solar and volcanic forcings would likely have produced *cooling*. Observed patterns of warming and their changes are simulated only by models that include anthropogenic forcings.' Further, in Africa by 2020, 'between 75 and 250 million people are projected to be exposed to increased water stress due to climate change' and 'in some countries, yields from rain-fed agriculture could be reduced by up to 50 per cent'.[48]

These problems are real, but solutions are not going to be found quicker if we see the issue as being essentially one of humanity versus nature. Indeed, such mistaken ways of framing the problem can positively get in the way. For example, many Greens are temperamentally averse to any kind of technological fix. They have become so used to thinking about the problem as being caused by our disrespect for nature that they see the only solutions as coming from humanity 'interfering' less and less with nature.

This is most evident in the case of genetically modified (GM) crops. The questions here concern threats to biodiversity (which raise separate questions as to the importance of biodiversity), human health, and the livelihoods of farmers and those who depend on them. These risks are almost certainly overstated. The government's chief scientific officer Sir John Beddington has said that 'GM crops have already demonstrated benefits in increasing yields and decreasing losses from pests and diseases, and are being grown globally in an increasing trend.'[49] His office has also talked about the need to 'to lower the ideological barriers between organic and GM, and thus fully exploit the combined potential of both GM crops and organic modes of production in order to achieve sustainable intensification of food production'.[50] But he has repeatedly complained that it is impossible to have a proper debate about these issues, since positions have become so polarized, with many ideologically opposed to GM crops. Beddington agrees that there is a vital need to assess the risks of new technologies, but this task is not made any easier by considering the irrelevant question of how far humans should be meddling with nature.

A proper understanding of nature is not, therefore, something that existed before science and technology set out to change the world: it was what came into being when we realized science was possible. The key difference is not between science, technology and nature but between nature – the world we can understand and change – and the supernatural world of myth and fantasy. It is therefore science which is most intimately connected with the very idea of nature, not a mythical untarnished time before science and technology.

What are we harming?

It is perhaps ironic that in viewing nature as something that humanity can harm, people are actually setting humanity aside from nature rather than seeing us as just another part of it. This way of thinking is most misleading in the way in which it encourages us to take a view of what we do in which

nature is the victim and we are aggressors. Not only am I
convinced this is wrong, it is arguably not even possible. We
can, of course, harm particular species. But we cannot harm
nature itself, nor can we help it. Let me explain what I mean.

Imagine that we are in a world in which, for entirely
natural reasons, the planet is cooling, rapidly. Unless we do
something fast, by 2050, large parts of the world will be
frozen over, with agriculture impossible. Something like
normal life will be possible between the tropics, but food
shortages and mass migration will become realities, with
devastating consequences. In such a situation it seems
obvious what we should do: dig up the coal, burn fossil
fuels, cut down the rainforests, get cows producing as much
methane as possible, ditch the bike and drive a gas-guzzler.
Man-made global warming would be a moral imperative,
not a disaster.

What this scenario shows is that there is nothing inherently immoral in how we live today. It is immoral only
because, for contingent reasons, it is going to make life in
the future very tough. Slavery, racism and sexism, in
contrast, are inherently immoral. You might be able to
devise some improbable thought experiment where each
became temporarily necessary, but in that case you'd simply
have come up with a scenario where it was a lesser evil. In
the cooling world example, having a big carbon footprint is
not a lesser evil – it is not an evil at all.

Now you might want to argue that this is not true, that all the things I described are wrong in themselves. This is roughly the 'deep green' position. But it is not one that many find at all compelling, and it is not the basis upon which, currently, most people judge us to be going wrong. Such a position would have to argue that the destruction of rainforests and so forth was wrong in itself. But why? The answer would have to be some version of the principle that we have no right to destroy elements of the planet, natural habitats and so forth.

This kind of argument always ends up impaled on a two-horned dilemma. If we suppose that the loss of habitat and so on is just wrong in itself, we are left with the odd conclusion that nature is wrong in itself. Over time, habitats completely change, and species die out. For example, 99.99 per cent of all species that have ever lived are now extinct.

The alternative is that these things are not wrong when they occur naturally, but are wrong when we speed them up, or change the course of nature. This is absurd for several reasons. First of all, we are part of nature, and in that sense the ways in which we change the environment are no less natural than the ways in which other species do. And other species really can totally transform environments. Think of how locusts can strip thousands of square miles of vegetation.

It is no use saying that this is different, because, in nature, things have evolved so that everything ends up in equilibrium.

If that is true, we cannot make it otherwise. Nature will also adapt to whatever we do. It may do so in ways which reduce biodiversity or even wipe us out, but it is not nature that is harmed by this, but us.

Even if we do allow for the spurious distinction between humans and nature, why is it OK if changes are natural and not if they are human-made? Cause seems irrelevant. What matters is whether changes are good or bad, and there is just no way to make sense of things being good or bad for the planet. The planet just is. For billions of years before humans came along it existed with no life, and will probably exist for billions more years after we've died out too. Far from making us humble, the idea that we have the power to hurt the earth is hubristic. From the hypothetical perspective of the earth (since, lacking consciousness, it has no perspective) we are at worst a temporary itch on something bigger and incomprehensibly longer-lived than ourselves. Nature doesn't care what we do because it doesn't have any thoughts or feelings, but it would not care even if it did.

Whose environment?

I have argued that to think of environmental issues in terms of the wrongs of human beings harming the planet is fundamentally mistaken. What's more, it is a mistake with potentially serious practical and moral repercussions. It would be grossly immoral to allow romanticism about nature to allow us to favour the environment over the people who live in it. The overriding question we need to ask when considering GMOs, nuclear power, global warming, the ozone layer or any other issue where nature is seen to be in need of protecting is: how is sentient life, and human beings especially, going to be affected? The problem with global warming is not that the planet suffers but that people do, through floods, water shortage or famine. It would surely therefore be wrong if we allowed our desire to safeguard nature to lead us to put plants before people.

In that sense, what we need to protect is not *the* environment but *our* environment. What matters is keeping the planet hospitable to human life. It may seem as though respect for nature for nature's sake is a worthy value which can only do us good. But it can in fact lead us badly astray.

Are we responsible for our actions?

Criminality and being in your right mind

It would appear to be a self-evident principle of justice that you are only to blame for what you intentionally do on the basis of what we could reasonably be assumed to have known at the time. If in all good faith you thought a gun was a toy but when you fired it, you killed someone, then you would not be considered guilty of murder. If you made no reasonable effort to check if the gun was a toy or real, however, you would be responsible for your ignorance. But does this apparently simple principle stand up to the complexities of real life?

On Sunday, 29 November 2004, Patrick O'Dwyer woke up with what was to prove the worst hangover of his – and his whole family's – life. The previous evening his 17-year-old sister Marguerite had taken advantage of the absence of their parents and thrown a party. He had got very drunk, thrown up, fallen over and had to be put to bed by his friends. Deeply embarrassed, he nonetheless went to work as an apprentice butcher as usual.

That evening, after watching television with Marguerite for a while he got up, went into the kitchen and returned with a hammer. The six blows he delivered to his sister's head were described by the pathologist as 'fatal and irrecoverable'. He then went back to the kitchen, picked up a pair of scissors and a knife and stabbed Marguerite 90 times in the neck, trunk and legs.

However, standing trial, his family was there to support him, and his mother asked the judge not to send him to jail, claiming he had 'no control over the events of that night'. He was, however, sentenced to six years for manslaughter on the grounds of diminished responsibility.

O'Dwyer had described how, at work that day he felt as though he were drifting into another world. When he initially picked up the hammer he said that his intention was to bash his own brains out. Instead, feeling 'it was like watching a video', he approached his sister, who looked at him and smiled before he delivered the fatal blows. He then went for a walk, came back to his bedroom, wrote 'Butcher Boy' on the wall with blood he had drawn from his arm with a scalpel, hit himself four times on the head with the hammer and slept until nearly noon the next day. Waking up and realizing what he had done, he at first tried to drown himself in the bath before turning himself in to the police.

Defence psychiatrists concluded that O'Dwyer had been suffering from 'depersonalization disorder'. Feelings of depersonalization include a sense that the world around you is not real or that your actions are not your own, as though you are observing yourself from the outside. It's often triggered by a traumatic experience. Many people have such feelings at some point, but when they are persistent or repeated, psychiatrists diagnose it as a mental disorder. In O'Dwyer's case, the diagnosis was enough for the judge to decide O'Dwyer was partly, but not fully, responsible for his actions. 'Diminished responsibility means exactly what it says,' said Justice Paul Carney. 'It reduces it, but does not extinguish it.' Had he accepted O'Dwyer's mother's claim that he had had no control, he would have been acquitted on the grounds of insanity, considered not responsible at all.[51]

O'Dwyer's case is disturbing but not only for the obvious reasons. If you start to think about why he was not considered to be fully to blame, it's easy to start sliding down a slippery slope in which no one is responsible for anything. And if that's the case, don't ethics and morality become a huge pretence?

Illness and ignorance

As well as the notion of intention, mentioned earlier, there is also a legal principle known as *ignorantia juris non excusat*: ignorance of the law is no excuse. The law would be unenforceable if anyone can plead innocent to anything on the basis that they didn't know what the law was.

So blame requires intention and knowledge. But this raises a problem which Socrates describes in Plato's *Meno*. As he put it in somewhat elliptical fashion, wrongdoers 'desire what they suppose to be goods although they are really evils; and if they are mistaken and suppose the evils to be goods they really desire goods'.[52] The basic idea is that if you desire something and choose to do it, it must be because you think it is good. You might recognize that it is illegal or thought to be bad by others, but you must see it as acceptable or else you wouldn't do it. Even murderers must think that either their victim deserves to be killed or that they are justified in sacrificing them for some greater good. In short, no one ever knowingly does what is wrong.

As Socrates made clear, this does not mean that anything anyone chooses really is good. On the contrary, we are often mistaken. But it makes all the difference in the world to how we treat wrongdoers because people who make mistakes need to be corrected and taught what is right, they do not deserve to be punished. Punishment is for wickedness and depravity, not for ignorance that is not self-inflicted. So while it may be true that *ignorantia juris non excusat,* it would seem true that *ignorantia moralis excusat*: ignorance of morality *is* an excuse.

This argument may seem less plausible in cases of relatively minor wrongdoing. So, for example, you might think that we know full well that theft might be wrong but we are simply too tempted by the rewards to resist. But in the case of really serious, violent crime, this viewpoint is actually very close to conventional wisdom. When we hear about stories like that of Patrick O'Dwyer we say things like 'no one in their right mind would do such a thing' or 'he's sick'. Indeed, there are some crimes where it seems that by definition, you can't be 'right in the head' if you did them. But if someone has a kind of illness or mental defect, that is not their fault. You might as well punish someone who is blind for not following the safety instructions on a sign and causing an accident.

Between illness and ignorance, then, it might look as though every really nasty crime is covered. One way or another, the 'criminals' either didn't know what they were doing or, as O'Dwyer's mother put it, were simply not in control of themselves. So, does that mean no one is really responsible for their crimes?

As I have already suggested, the idea that no one ever knowingly does wrong does not seem to fit experience. The reason it might appear this way to some philosophers is perhaps because they tend to imagine that logic and our actual mental processes are more related than they are. It would indeed be a paradox if we wanted to do what was best, understood that the best for us was also what was right, and did wrong nonetheless. But it is not self-evident that what is best for us is also what is right, so there seems to be no contradiction in someone wanting to do what is best for them while also believing it is wrong. What's more, if psychology has taught us anything it's that our minds are a whirl of contradictory and conflicting beliefs and desires and that decision-making is not based on a logical resolution of these tensions. Sometimes, for instance, the emotional side of us is just more powerful than the rational side, and so we go with what we want at that moment rather than with what, on reflection, we think is best, all things considered. So although we may *sometimes* do wrong because we are not aware of what is right, it seems implausible to suggest that we are *always* ignorant when we act immorally.

The case of illness is more complicated. In law, a verdict of diminished responsibility through insanity would be made on the basis of the reports of one or more psychiatric reports. In other words, the law defers to expert opinion on what constitutes mental illness. Although it seems obvious that it could hardly do anything else, from a justice point of view this is deeply problematic. The trouble is that psychiatric diagnoses are highly controversial. Whereas there are usually very clear, internationally accepted definitions of bodily diseases and ailments, the list and diagnostic criteria for mental disorders varies and changes over time and between jurisdictions. Internationally, many take a lead from the *Diagnostic and Statistical Manual of Mental Disorders (DSM)* of the American Psychiatric Association. To describe this as controversial is something of an understatement. Its claim to objective authority is undermined by the historical fact that it included homosexuality as a psychiatric disease until 1973. With each new edition (the fifth is pending), the number of recognized conditions increases and the criteria for diagnosing many of the existing ones changes. What this illustrates is that whether one is considered to have a mental illness that diminishes the ability to make responsible choices or not depends a great deal on who you ask and when. There is no simple definition.

Although this flags up a problem with the use of psychiatric diagnoses in attributions of responsibility, it does not provide a fatal objection. All we need do is accept that responsibility is a matter of degree, which is precisely what the use of the term 'diminished' in the law suggests. That being the case, it is to be expected that there will be grey areas and indeed some mistakes made in deciding how responsible a person is. It does not undermine the basic idea that there is a normal capacity for making responsible choices and that this can be impaired by mental disorders.

No more normal?

Where things get a little murkier is when you ask why it is that a mental disorder is supposed to deprive us of responsibility. The standard answer would be that there is such a thing as normal cognitive functioning – normal decision-making, thinking, reflection and so on – and that when someone has a mental illness, these functions do not work properly. Robbed of our ability to think straight, we can no longer be considered fully responsible.

With advances in neuroscience, we are used to thinking about these dysfunctions in terms of changes in the brain, hence the glib précis of the diminished responsibility plea: 'my brain made me do it'. But we should remember that the idea of diminished responsibility pre-dates fMRI (functional magnetic resonance imaging) scans and all the other advances that enable us to know what exactly is going on in the brain when someone fails to foresee consequences, for example, or loses their sense of self. Impaired cognitive function can be diagnosed simply by observing and testing how people think, it need not involve identifying the neural underpinning of this.

Nonetheless, the problem any appeal to diminished cognitive function has for ideas of responsibility are made clearest by considering those cases where it is attributed to brain dysfunction. So, for example, consider the case of

O'Dwyer's depersonalization disorder. It might be explained that this was the result of his prefrontal cortex inhibiting the usual array of emotional responses that facilitate the kind of empathetic understanding that makes us see that hitting someone with a hammer is going to hurt them. Although this is not yet properly understood, suggestions that it is related to abnormal levels of cortisol and dysregulation of the hypothalamic-pituitary-adrenal axis give some flavour of what a fuller explanation would look like. All this sounds as though it clearly places responsibility for O'Dwyer's actions on the defective brain processes, not O'Dwyer himself.

But wait a minute. What happens when someone who does not have depersonalization disorder makes his decisions? We could describe this as involving the prefrontal cortex allowing the usual array of emotional responses that facilitate empathetic understanding in a brain operating with normal cortisol levels and a regulated hypothalamic-pituitary-adrenal axis. In this case, ordinary, functional brain processes underlie the decisions made. But the critical thing is, whether a brain is normal or pathological, in both cases you can describe the underlying neural basis of the decision. It is not the case that in one situation 'my brain made me do it' but in the other it didn't. What else powers thought than the brain? Healthy or not, our brains always 'made us do it', if by that we mean that all thought and decision-making is in some sense dependent on brain function (which surely it is). It seems the insanity defence starts us down a slippery slope that ends in the valley of determinism, the denial of free will.

So why is it in one case we are considered responsible and in the other we are not? How we answer this question is critical. Some would argue that, if all decisions are purely the result of brain function, there is no way to make sense of the idea that healthy brains are more capable of making free choices than unhealthy ones. In every case, it is ultimately brains that produce decisions and actions. If these are anti-social or dangerous, we may have to do something about it. But even if this requires us to place legal blame on people, moral blame goes out of the window.

There is no easy answer to this troubling conclusion. There is, however, a difficult one. Compatibilism is the view that although we must accept that every choice we make, every thought we have, is in some sense the product of the never-ending chain of physical causes and effects that ultimately play out at the level of our bodies and brains, but that, nonetheless, there are some important senses in which we are free. How precisely this is argued in different theories varies, but the general approach is to deny the assumption that for a choice to be free its originating cause must be our own, uncaused choice. The fact that we can always trace decisions to causes such as brain events, genetic inheritance or environmental prompts is not fatal to free will. All that matters is that the choice is made on the basis of our own, unhindered cognitive resources, based as they are on neural processes.

On this view, in neurological terms, to be free can be described as having a brain with the capacity to generate choices and actions unhindered by malfunction or external constraint or coercion. On first pass this might seem deeply unsatisfactory. Whether mentally ill or not, the brain can always be said to generate its own actions and choices. Isn't the stipulation that they are normal, healthy and unimpeded arbitrary? Doesn't it boil down to saying that free simply means normal?

Not quite. What matters here is that we have the capacity to *self-regulate*. Of course, if thought depends on the brain, then this capacity is ultimately going to be given a neurological explanation. But whatever turned out to be the engine of thought, something had to be, even if it were an immaterial soul. And what would make that something free would not be some mysterious ability to initiate a chain of causes all by itself, but its ability to regulate itself.

So, for example, consider the difference between O'Dwyer and someone else who is severely depressed and, ashamed, has picked up a hammer with the thought of harming themselves, and feels instead a fleeting urge to hit his sister with it. In both cases, if we delved into their brains, all we would see was neurons firing in different regions of the brain. Nothing would tell us that one was free and the other was not. But there is a crucial difference. The neural firings in the merely depressed person are such that the mind is able to see what it is doing, notice that it is wrong and stop. Encouragement, punishment, reading moral philosophy and the like can all make a difference to what that self-regulating system decides. For O'Dwyer, none of this was true. He had lost the crucial power of self-regulation.

So despite the grey area between mental order and disorder, there does seem to be a defensible rationale for the law's provision of diminished responsibility. Whether we want to call it illness or simply dysfunction, it should make a difference to how we deal with criminals.

I said that this is only the sketch of a proper answer and clearly much more needs to be said to make it complete. But it seems that this is the only general kind of answer that can promise to defeat the objection that our brains always make us do it, and so nobody is ever responsible. Free will has to be understood not in some ultimate sense in which we could have done anything we wanted, uncaused by our brains, bodies, heredity and environment. Indeed, it seems hard to imagine what such a free will could even be. Rather, if we have any free will at all, it must be of a more limited kind, an ability to regulate our behaviours for ourselves. The point of holding people responsible for their actions is not, therefore, that we think they could have done otherwise or that ultimately brain processes don't explain what they did. We hold people responsible because to do so is to reinforce the human capacity to be a self-regulating individual. That may not quite be what most people have in mind when they think about what it means to be free and responsible. But that may be no bad thing, if what they do have in mind is actually vague at best and incoherent at worst.

What is a just war?
The rights and wrongs of armed conflict

What makes the difference between a good war and a bad one? Almost uniquely in philosophy, there is a theoretical framework for answering this question which is widely, if not universally, shared. Even more remarkably, the basic form of Just War Theory is pretty much the same as that first articulated by Thomas Aquinas in the 13th century.[53]

On 7 October 2001, America, Britain and Australia launched the first air strikes in their military campaign in Afghanistan. Working with the Afghan United Front (also known as the Northern Alliance), the aim of Operation Enduring Freedom was to topple the Taliban regime which, in the words of the then British Prime Minister Tony Blair, 'harboured and supported' al-Qaeda terrorists.

'None of the leaders involved in this action want war,' Blair said that day. 'But we know that sometimes to safeguard peace, we have to fight. . . . We only do it if the cause is just. This cause is just.' Over the Atlantic, his counterpart George W. Bush told his military servicemen and women, 'Your mission is defined; your objectives are clear; your goal is just.'

Nearly 18 months later, on 20 March 2003, Blair was again addressing the nation to announce the start of a war. 'On Tuesday night I gave the order for British forces to take part in military action in Iraq.' But among the differences between this announcement and the one about Afghanistan was an acknowledgement that this campaign was much more controversial. Barack Obama, for example, who inherited both campaigns when he took office as US president in 2009, had opposed the Iraq War but supported the Afghan one. Among democrats Iraq became known as the 'bad war' and Afghanistan 'the good war'. In both cases, the principles invoked to defend and attack the use of military action were all to be found in Just War Theory.

The principles

Although Just War Theory (JWT) is often talked about in the singular, there is in fact no canonical version of its central principles. Different versions add or omit certain clauses and elaborate on them in different ways. Nevertheless, there are several principles which provide the common bulk of the theory in all its versions. These principles are divided into two categories. Those of *jus ad bellum* concern the rightness (*jus*) of going to war (*bellum*), while those of *jus in bello* deal with moral conduct in a war.

The central criteria of *jus ad bellum* are, first, that the cause is just, meaning that intervention is required to protect life from imminent and grave danger. The clearest example of such a just cause is self-defence. Second, there has to be right intention, usually meaning the end of killing and the establishment of peace. A just cause does not necessarily entail right intention. A nation may use the fact that there is a grave danger to life as a pretext to seize territory, for example. This would be to bring the wrong intention to a just cause.

Third, the war needs to be waged by a competent, legitimate authority. Fourth, there must be a good probability of success, otherwise the inevitable loss of life would be wasted. Fifth, war must always be the last resort. And sixth, the use of military force must be proportionate. If a huge invading army is sent in to deal with something a dozen soldiers could have sorted out, the war cannot be just.

Once the war has started, principles of *jus in bello* need to be followed. Here, the main principles can be grouped under two headings. First, all actions must respect a proper distinction between combatants and non-combatants. Included under this we might place the humane treatment of prisoners of war. Second, all individual actions in the war have to be proportionate. This means using the minimum force required by military necessity. It also means avoiding actions *malum in se*, meaning 'bad in themselves', such as rape, use of weapons whose effects cannot be controlled, torture and so on.

In summary then, we could define the key principles of Just War Theory thus:

JUS AD BELLUM	JUS IN BELLO
Just cause	Respect for non-combatants
Right intention	Minimum force
Legitmate authority	
Probability of success	
Last resort	
Proportionality	

At first sight, these principles might appear to be both reasonable and capable of providing a kind of checklist against which the rightness of a war could be judged. But on reflection we might conclude that the very reason the list looks so sensible is that none of the criteria is specific enough to actually provide a clear test of whether it has been fulfilled. The wars in Iraq and Afghanistan illustrate this very well.

Just war in Afghanistan?

Consider then first of all how the terms of Just War Theory were used to justify the war in Afghanistan. In his statement of 7 October 2001, Tony Blair's last words boldly asserted that the first condition of JWT was fulfilled: 'This cause is just.' Earlier he gave his reasons, which was that,

> the al-Qaeda network threatens Europe, including Britain, and indeed any nation throughout the world that does not share their fanatical views. So we have a direct interest in acting in our self-defence to protect British lives.

Regarding the second criteria of intention, on the same day, addressing the American people, George W. Bush said, 'These carefully targeted actions are designed to disrupt the use of Afghanistan as a terrorist base of operations, and to attack the military capability of the Taliban regime.' He also claimed legitimate authority, pointing to widespread international backing and saying 'We are supported by the collective will of the world.' And he expressed no doubt that the mission would be successful: 'Peace and freedom will prevail.'

Both Bush and Blair made it clear that they believed no other option was available to them and this was the last resort. 'It is more than two weeks since an ultimatum was delivered to the Taliban to yield up the terrorists or face the consequences,' said Blair. 'It is clear beyond doubt that the Taliban will not do this.' And although there were inevitably dangers, Blair insisted that this large-scale war was proportionate to the risks it was addressing.

The world understands that whilst of course there are dangers in acting as we are . . . the dangers of inaction are far, far greater – the threat of further such outrages, the threats to our economies, the threat to the stability of the world.

Both leaders also offered reassurances that their conduct in the coming war would meet the conditions of *jus in bello*. They were particularly keen to stress their desire not just to protect non-combatants, but to actively help them. 'As we strike military targets, we will also drop food, medicine and supplies to the starving and suffering men and women and children of Afghanistan,' said Bush. And, finally, they both emphasized the 'targeted' nature of all attacks, thus acknowledging the imperative for all force to be proportionate.

Those who disagreed with the war could not therefore claim that the leaders ignored the demands of Just War Theory. On the contrary, they explicitly addressed all of them. Perhaps it was because of the apparent fundamental justness of the cause – that the Taliban's nurturing of al-Qaeda presented a real threat to British and American citizens, one which had already taken lives on 9/11 – that the campaign received so much initial support. Many also accepted that the intention was as stated, unlike the First Gulf War where people suspected the emergence of a just cause – the liberation of Kuwait – was the pretext for an intended oil-grab.

The reason there is still room to dispute the legitimacy of the war is simply that many, if not all, of the leaders' claims surrounding the justice of the campaign are open to dispute. Was it really a proportionate, last-resort action with a high degree of probability of achieving its goal? That is a question whose answer is not even clear today, when with the benefit of hindsight we can see what has actually happened. Around 400 British and 1,500 American soldiers have died, along with around 15,000 civilians (although there are nothing like definitive figures available here). The financial cost of the war is also hard to quantify, but even Barack Obama put the total figure for the US at around $1 trillion. Although the stated aims do seem to have been achieved, as Western forces were preparing to leave it was not at all clear that a sustainable peace has been put in its place and nor that the Taliban has been more than temporarily frustrated. As for whether the point of last resort had truly been reached, Blair himself acknowledged at the start of the campaign that there was 'at present no specific credible threat to the United Kingdom that we know of'.

It could be argued that the mere fact that it is not clear whether these criteria of JWT have been met means that, in effect, they have not. For a war to be just, you need to be able to answer each question posed by JWT with a clear yes. With the stakes so high, 'maybe' or 'I think so' isn't good enough. So even if things do work out for the best, it can still be wrong to start a conflict when the outcomes are too uncertain.

On the other hand, it can also be argued that when stakes are very high you have to try, even if you cannot say you will probably succeed. No one could have been sure in 1939, for example, that the allies would have prevailed over the Third Reich. But most would agree that it had to be worth the effort: it was simply not an option to give up against so great an evil.

So JWT does not provide a clear answer to the rightness of war, even in a case where most people did think it was justified. And it becomes even less capable of providing authority in a much more controversial campaign.

Just war in Iraq?

Although the Iraq War faced much more opposition from the electorates of the countries involved, both George W. Bush and Tony Blair provided justifications for its legitimacy that covered all the criteria of Just War Theory. First and foremost, Bush told the American people on 20 March 2003, announcing the start of military action, that there was a just cause for the war: 'to disarm Iraq, to free its people and to defend the world from grave danger'. He was also at pains to stress that this cause provided the sole and right intention for the action. 'We have no ambition in Iraq except to remove a threat and restore control of that country to its own people,' he said. In Britain, Blair was telling his nation the same thing, claiming that 'I have never put our justification for action as regime change.' Blair maintained that 'we have to act within the terms set out in [United Nations] resolution 1441'. It was that resolution that gave the action legitimate authority, 'our legal base', as Blair put it.

As in Afghanistan, Bush expressed confidence that the action had a high probability of success, saying 'We will bring freedom to others and we will prevail.' Both leaders knew that many people did not think that the world had reached the stage where this was the last resort and Blair in particular aimed to counter such a view. 'Our fault has not been impatience,' he had told Parliament two days earlier. 'The truth is our patience should have been exhausted weeks and months and years ago.'[54]

As he announced that British forces had begun their actions, Blair also set out the case for why this use of over-whelming force was nonetheless proportionate to the grave danger:

Should terrorists obtain these weapons now being manu-factured and traded around the world the carnage they could inflict to our economies, to our security, to world peace would be beyond our most vivid imagination. My

judgement as prime minister is that this threat is real,
growing and of an entirely different nature to any conven-
tional threat to our security that Britain has faced before.

Just as was the case 18 months earlier in Afghanistan,
both premiers took the opportunity to pledge that the
conduct of their forces during the war would also be just. 'I
want Americans and all the world to know that coalition
forces will make every effort to spare innocent civilians
from harm,' said Bush, even though the adversary Saddam
Hussein 'has placed Iraqi troops and equipment in civilian
areas, attempting to use innocent men, women and children as shields for his own military.' Action would be firm
but proportionate. 'Now that conflict has come, the only
way to limit its duration is to apply decisive force,' he said.

But the fact that both Bush and Blair ticked off the criteria
of JWT to their own satisfaction did not mean they had
truly been fulfilled. In this case, the gravest doubts were
over the justness of the cause and the issue of last resort. As
we have seen, Bush summed up the just cause case as being
the need 'to disarm Iraq, to free its people and to defend the
world from grave danger'. But, as it turned out, Iraq did not
need disarming as it simply didn't have the weapons of mass
destruction that many believed it had. This does not mean
the war was necessarily started under false pretences. When
Blair said on 20 March 2003 that 'UN weapons inspectors

say vast amounts of chemical and biological poisons such as anthrax, VX nerve agent and mustard gas remain unaccounted for in Iraq', there is no reason to think he did not do so in good faith. 'Unaccounted for' does not mean 'present', of course, but Blair argued he could not afford to have taken that risk. Once again, it seems a critical issue whether an unequivocal 'yes' is needed to the questions posed by JWT or whether a balance of evidence is enough. These doubts over the need to disarm Iraq obviously lead to doubts over whether there really was a need to lead an invasion in order 'to defend the world from grave danger', since it suggests that danger was not so grave after all. And all this makes the case for the action being a last resort much less convincing.

One of the most controversial aspects of the case for the war against Iraq being just comes from the extent to which its aim was 'to free its people'. First of all, no matter what we think of that goal, it would not seem to be one that legitimized outside interference. UN Resolution 1441, for instance, clearly did not sanction military action on those grounds. Nor does standard JWT allow this as a just cause, unless there is imminent and grave danger to the citizens of a country. It could be countered, however, that there have been several military interventions by outside powers – most notably in the former Yugoslavia and Sierra Leone – which have been widely supported as just wars and yet did not seem to fit the criteria of JWT either in terms of the cause or in the action having the backing of international law to provide the legitimate authority. Does this show the wars were not so moral after all, or that JWT fails to account for all cases of just warfare?

There are also severe doubts over whether the action was proportionate, with a sufficiently high degree of probability of success. Iraq Body Count puts the number of civilian deaths as a result of the conflict at over 100,000, a number similar to other credible estimates.[55] Over 4,400 US soldiers have died in the conflict, along with over 300 from other coalition forces, including nearly 200 from Britain. Was this a proportionate price to pay for the gains? Of course, many believe it was not. But it should be clear that there simply is no straightforward, factual answer to this. The people most affected, Iraqis themselves, don't all agree. For all the horrors, even with the benefit of hindsight, many would not choose to roll the tape back and see what would have happened had Saddam Hussein not been forced from power. Others think the price is obviously too high.

As with Afghanistan, no matter what we think of what actually happened, it could still be argued that the uncertainty at the outset as to what the outcome would be alone means that the war was unjustified. If there was confidence that the mission would be a success, that was misplaced. It was always going to be possible that the result would be a quagmire, a bloody civil war, or the replacement of one monstrous regime with another.

Deliberately or not, both Bush and Blair justified both actions in terms which appear to come straight from Just War Theory. But in at least one of those conflicts, the majority opinion seems to be that the war was not justified at all. That is possible because the Just War Theory provides no more than a key set of considerations: it does not provide clear criteria with which to assess whether a war really is just. There is always a need for interpretation, both of the principles and the facts on the ground at the time. But what's more, we cannot treat Just War Theory as though it were written authoritatively forever on tablets of stone. If what is right seems to contradict or not be covered by Just War Theory, we cannot assume the theory must prevail.

Is torture always wrong?
How to stop a ticking bomb

The argument for torture is often taken to be a straightforward utilitarian one: by sacrificing the interests of one, guilty person, you save the lives of many more innocents. The ledger of losses and gains in terms of welfare, happiness or whatever other ultimate good we use to assess the rightness of actions would clearly show a substantial gain. Does such a justification work?

It's 11 September 2001 and Americans are glued to their television sets amazed at what they are watching. Overnight, the FBI have arrested 19 men whom they say were about to launch an unprecedented terrorist attack on the country that could have left tens of thousands dead. Pictures show Mohamed Atta, Waleed al-Shehri, Wail al-Shehri and seven others being taken from Logan International Airport in Boston into police custody. Incredibly, their plan was to hijack aircraft and use them as flying missiles, crashing them into the twin towers of New York's World Trade Center. Other arrests have been made at Newark International Airport, New Jersey, and Dulles International Airport, Washington DC, where plotters intended to hijack and crash aircraft into the White House and the Pentagon respectively.

The images switch to President George W. Bush who has convened a press conference at the E. Booker Elementary School in Sarasota County, Florida. He pays tribute to the security services for foiling a plot that, had it been carried out, would have left many children, like the ones he would be reading a story to later, orphans.

In this alternative history, 49-year-old Maria Rose Abad, senior vice president of Keefe, Bruyette & Woods, is not the first name in the list of the 2,977 victims of 9/11, and 29-year-old Igor Zukelman is not the last. Rather they are just two of many people who, on watching the news, had a terrifying sense of how close they came to death.

But this is not a simple story of lives saved and pain prevented. Only 24 hours before, all the FBI knew was that a major terrorist attack was planned somewhere in the USA and that the man they had captured, Khalid Sheikh Mohammed, knew exactly what that plan was. But unless he revealed the truth to them very quickly, they could do nothing to prevent it. Many, perhaps including the families of Abad and Zukelman, are therefore glad that interrogators ignored the Geneva Conventions and the United Nations Convention against Torture and Other Cruel, Inhuman or Degrading Treatment or Punishment. As they saw it, one would-be mass murderer had an excruciating few hours of pain, but thousands of innocent people had their lives saved, and tens of thousands of friends and relatives were spared untold shock and grief.

This is a version of one of the most notorious thought experiments in moral philosophy: the 'ticking bomb' scenario, in which the only way to obtain life-saving information fast is by torture. The 'what if?' is intended to challenge the idea that torture is always wrong in all circumstances, an absolutist stance enshrined in international law. But when presented with ticking bomb cases, many find it hard to justify a blanket prohibition. If we really could have saved all those lives on 9/11 by torturing Khalid Sheikh Mohammed, wouldn't it have simply been a kind of moral squeamishness not to do so? Would the FBI really have kept their hands clean by refusing to do so, or would it have been the blood of the 9/11 victims that they could not have washed off?

The case for torture

One criticism of the argument that torture is justified by its beneficial effects is that it is essentially based on probabilities: when it is overwhelmingly probable that one course of action has a much better outcome than another, we should follow the former. But if all that is needed is for the pain balance sheet to come out positive in the long run – even if routine torture would cause more suffering than it prevented, the utilitarian calculus could be used to justify torture in any case where it seems that it will save a few lives, not only when it is the only hope of saving many. This is not really an argument against torture, however. All it does is push the argument for torture to its logical conclusion. If you don't like where it ends up, then you have to show why the argument is wrong. Your unease is not a rebuttal.

One common response from people persuaded by the logic of the utilitarian argument but disturbed by its conclusions is to argue that torture doesn't actually work, so hypothetical cases where it does are beside the point. Facts are critical to this moral debate. Because the utilitarian argument works on the basis of probabilities, if it is unlikely that torture will elicit accurate information, then the moral case for using it weakens, whereas if torture is an effective means of getting accurate information, the utilitarian argument for its use is strengthened.

So does it work? It's very hard for an impartial observer to know because most reports of this seem to suffer from what psychologists call confirmation bias: the tendency to attend to evidence that fits your opinion and ignore or downplay evidence contrary to it. If you try to weigh up more impartial opinions, unfortunately they are not unanimous. Former head of the British intelligence service MI5 Eliza Manningham-Buller is against torture on moral grounds, so has no interest in talking up its efficacy. But she has said, 'It's not the case that torture always produces false information and actually it's clear that torture can contribute to saving lives, but I don't think that's the point.'[56] On the other hand, Ali Soufan, a former FBI interrogator who has witnessed 'enhanced interrogation' (which the US government does not consider torture but many critics do) has repeatedly said that it is 'ineffective and harmful to our national security'.[57]

If efficacy is not the point, as Manningham-Buller claims, what is? As we have already seen, many believe that some things are just wrong and they are not made right because they can be used to bring about a desirable end. But, interestingly, this is not the argument Manningham-Buller used to oppose torture. Although she said she did not believe it was 'something that is right, legal or moral to do', when she fleshed out her objections, they too hinged on consequences: it's simply that they were wider and longer-term ones than the immediate saving of lives. So, she said,

> I believe that the acquisition of short-term gain through water-boarding and other forms of mistreatment was a profound mistake and lost the United States moral authority and some of the widespread sympathy it had enjoyed as a result of 9/11. And I am confident that I know the answer to the question of whether torture has made the world a safer place. It hasn't.

Others have made similar arguments, saying that it creates sympathy for the terrorist groups and undermines the ability of the torturing state to occupy the moral high ground.

This is a version of the kind of subtler consequentialist argument we saw in the chapter *Do the Ends Justify the Means?* As such, it is still based on tallying costs and benefits. There is nothing here about the intrinsic wrongness of torture. Many find this disturbing. Even if a consequence-based argument concluded there was never going to be a conceivable real-world situation where torture would be OK, the fact that it is not ruled out *in principle* seems to be wrong. Surely, it is thought, the morality of this issue cannot boil down simply to a question of whether or not it is effective?

One line of thought that suggests it is not, follows one of the definitions of torture used in international law: 'cruel, inhuman, or degrading treatment'. To a lesser or greater degree, each of these words suggests a wrongness that is not conditional on circumstances. To be 'cruel', for example, is to inflict pain or suffering either unnecessarily or for the reason that it is pain or suffering, not simply because it is required to achieve some desired goal. Such actions must surely always be wrong. We can accept that sometimes we might deliberately cause pain in the service of some more worthwhile goal, such as amputating a limb without anaesthetic as the only way to prevent gangrene spreading. Such actions can never be called cruel, however, since cruelty is the infliction of more suffering than is justified.

'Degrading' behaviour would also always appear to be wrong, implying as it does the reduction of something to a status lower than it should have. Medical patients can feel humiliated or degraded if they become incontinent and incapacitated, needing to be cleaned up by others. But we would not accuse the people charged with these tasks of humiliating or degrading them. We would only say that, if they acted in such a way as to unnecessarily exacerbate whatever feelings of humiliation patients would have. Like 'cruel', 'degrading' is a term that implies an excess and so is by definition wrong.

Finally 'inhuman' implies treatment without possible justification. It's a word that evokes Kant's injunction to 'act that you use humanity, whether in your own person or in the person of any other, always at the same time as an end, never merely as a means'.[58] This should not be surprising, since Kant is the leading moral philosopher in the deontological tradition, which maintains the rightness and wrongness of actions independent of their consequences.

It would then seem as though 'cruel, inhuman, or degrading treatment' is of its nature wrong, whether it brings about more welfare or happiness, or not. But this could be more of a linguistic truth than a moral one. If you use terms that imply wrongness, then, of course, to apply them to something is to declare that they are wrong. But all that means is that you are making your moral judgement in your description, not that the moral judgement simply arises out of the plain facts. We can either define torture in such a way that does not presume it to be right or wrong, and then ask if it is ever morally justified. Or we can define it in such a way that by definition it is wrong, and then ask if a particular form of 'enhanced interrogation' counts as torture. What we can't do is beg the question by defining something in such a way that it must be wrong and then claiming that this ends the debate.

Defenders of torture, say about cases such as the imaginary pre-9/11 torture of Khalid Sheikh Mohammed, would deny that it was cruel or degrading on the grounds that these words do not refer to the pain or humiliation a person feels but the intentions of the perpetrator. Given that those aims are to extract information, no more and no less, it would be argued the treatment was not cruel, since it only applied as much pain as was necessary, and nor was it degrading, because no matter how much degradation the interrogee felt, that was simply a foreseeable effect, not the intention. As for the claim that torture is inhuman, this could be dismissed as pure rhetoric, a means of expressing outrage without actually saying anything informative about what it is that is supposed to be outrageous. Indeed, the accusation could be turned around: is it not 'inhuman' to stand by and let innocent people be killed because of qualms about making a guilty person suffer?

This reflects a broader objection to the idea that torture is inherently wrong. The worry is that we may be too concerned with keeping our own hands clean and not enough with making sure that justice prevails. The tragedy of torture lies precisely in the fact that it requires us to do things we would never usually contemplate because the need to do so is over whelming. There is a kind of 'moral self-indulgence', as the late Bernard Williams put it, about refusing to do unsavoury things that are required to achieve a higher good.[59] If this is right, then it is conceivable that sometimes it may be necessary to humiliate someone, even treat them as less than fully human, if that is the only means of saving innocent lives.

A slightly different point – or perhaps an alternative way of seeing the same point – is to recognize the existence of what we might call moral tragedies. These are situations where we cannot avoid doing something wrong, and the best we can do is the least worse. So perhaps torture is degrading, because it needs to be able to crack a person's will. But no matter how awful it is to humiliate a person, it is preferable to seeing people blown to pieces. This is a way of accepting the deontological claim that some actions are wrong in themselves, but insisting that we sometimes need to do the lesser evil. In the torture case, the choice might be between failing to intervene to protect innocent life and treating someone in an inhuman way. Both things might be wrong, but whatever you do, you have to do one of them.

And faced with such a choice, it may be better to degrade one person than condemn more to death.

Never say never

You might think the discussion so far has been rather unbalanced, that the arguments against torture have been found more wanting than the defences of it. Given that most decent people do oppose torture, and more often than not without exception, this might seem to distort the moral consensus of the situation. In fact, in my view, it is precisely so that we can robustly oppose torture in the real world that we have to be so merciless in our dissection of arguments that try to establish an absolute prohibition on it.

To put my worry in more general terms, I think that misguided ways of thinking about ethics theoretically can be unhelpful when we come to think about it practically. One such mistake concerns the misplaced desire for *always* and *never*. It seems that we believe we need moral rules and that, furthermore, rules aren't really rules if they do not encompass exceptions. I think both assumptions are false. I'm not convinced we need moral rules at all. All we need in order to do the right thing is to be able to consider what the morally relevant factors are in a situation and have the intelligence and wisdom to weigh them up. But every situation is different so no rule can capture every conceivable instance.

The reason it seems natural to believe there are moral rules is that there are undoubtedly what we could call *moral patterns*. It is not coincidental, that similar circumstances lead us to the same kind of moral judgements. And so murder, infidelity, theft and so on are almost always wrong. But that doesn't establish rules like 'murder is wrong' and it certainly doesn't mean such actions are wrong because they break a moral rule. In that sense moral rules are more like laws of nature than laws of courts: they describe regularities found in nature, they do not prescribe regularities we ought to follow.

The misguided search for exceptionless moral rules therefore leads us to be too concerned by imaginary situations in which the usual patterns do not apply. We worry that the wrongness of torture is somehow undermined because we can conceive of strange cases where it might be permissible. But its wrongness never depended on their being an absolute rule against it. Its wrongness rather follows from what, in practice, it almost always involves.

The use of thought experiments in moral philosophy can exacerbate these problems, and add a few more. More often than not, thought experiments are designed with the specific aim of finding a counter-example to a generally accepted principle. This is thought important as it prompts us to reject or refine the principle or refine it. This can be useful, just as long as we remember that what we are reflecting or refining is merely an attempt to capture what different individual cases have in common. If we find that a principle doesn't fit the cases to which it is supposed to apply, that does not necessarily mean that we no longer have a reason to think of the situations that fall under the principle as wrong.

But what is perhaps most misleading about thought experiments is that they strip away the thick layers of context that make real-life situations so difficult and individual. They deliberately attempt to abstract from the real world, but because of this we should always be wary about applying the conclusions we draw from them back on to that real world.

So, in the case of torture, it would suggest that the question of whether it is always and necessarily wrong is a dangerous distraction. If we believe that, as a matter of fact, we cannot think of a single case where it was justified, we have every reason to put in place laws and rules that prohibit it. We create laws and inculcate habits that serve us well for the vast majority of the time, and we use our capacity to question and reflect to deal with any exceptions that come along. Maybe a day will come when someone is correct to judge that torture is indeed the only right thing to do. Knowing that is a possibility is no more reason to take a firm stand against torture than knowing it could be necessary to try to leap a deep ravine is a reason to jump off every high cliff you come across. There is a saying: hard cases make bad law. Perhaps hard cases can make bad ethics too.

What can science tell us about morality?
What facts tell us about values

Goodness is not an element located somewhere between Actinium and Thorium on the periodic table. Justice has no mass or velocity. Wickedness does not grow in anything other than a metaphorical way. These things are obviously true. And so it might seem equally obvious that if we want to know about morality, it is useless to look to science.

But for as long as there has been science there have been some who have believed it could be extended to explain ethics as well as electronics. And these people seem to have grown in number in recent years. Take, for example, the neuroscientist Sam Harris who subtitled one of his books *How Science Determines Human Values*. Not 'helps us to understand' or 'is relevant to' but 'determines'. Indeed, he argues that 'morality should be considered an undeveloped branch of science'. As he sees it, facts such as those about how thoughts and intentions arise in the brain and give rise to actions that affect others, 'exhaust what we can reasonably mean by terms like "good" and "evil"'.[60]

Harris is not the only one to have high hopes for what science can contribute to morality. There is now a whole research area known as evolutionary ethics which, in the words of Michael Ruse, claims that 'Morality is not some ethereal thing out there, like mathematics (assuming that this is true of mathematics). It is a very human thing and that means it is a Darwinian evolution thing.'[61] More specifically, 'It is an adaptation to get us to be sophisticated social animals.'[62]

Some go so far as to say that science shows that morality is an illusion. The philosopher of science Alex Rosenberg argues that scientism is the correct world view which cannot avoid the nihilistic conclusion 'that the whole idea of "morally permissible" is untenable nonsense.'[63]

However, there are equally vocal advocates of the opposite view. As the biologist Stephen Jay Gould put it,

> *Science can say nothing about the morality of morals. That is, the potential discovery by anthropologists that murder, infanticide, genocide, and xenophobia may have character- ized many human societies, may have arisen preferentially in certain social situations, and may even be adaptationally beneficial in certain contexts, offers no support whatever for the moral proposition that we ought to behave in such a manner.*[64]

For Gould, and many others, science and morality are distinct for the same reason that science and religion are. Science and religion have authority over two different 'magisteria' of thought. Science, says Gould, deals with 'the empirical realm: what the Universe is made of (fact) and why does it work in this way (theory). The magisterium of religion extends over questions of ultimate meaning and moral value. These two magisteria do not overlap, nor do they encompass all inquiry.'[65] Similarly, the physicist John Polkinghorne and the mathematician Nicholas Beale say 'Science is concerned with the question, How? – By what process do things happen? Theology is concerned with the question, Why? – Is there a meaning and purpose behind what is happening?'[66] In both cases what is true of ethics is true of religion: it deals with the realm of values, which science does not.

So, on the one hand we have those who claim science has nothing to say about ethics, because science is concerned with facts and ethics is about values. On the other, you have those who argue that science can fully explain – or perhaps even explain away – the whole of morality. Which side is right?

From *is* to *ought*

Those who argue for the strict division between science and morality often appeal to one of the key conceptual distinctions of modern philosophy: between *is* and *ought*, between *facts* and *values*. David Hume was the first to makes this plain. He described how he would be reading what appeared to be a straightforwardly factual text,

> when all of a sudden I am surprised to find, that instead of the usual copulations of propositions, is, *and* is not, I meet with no proposition that is not connected with an ought, *or an* ought not.

He describes this shift as 'imperceptible' but,

> some reason should be given; for what seems altogether inconceivable, how this new relation can be a deduction from others, which are entirely different from it.[67]

The key point is a simple and powerful one. It never follows from the mere fact that something *is* the case, that something *ought to be* the case. So, for example, the fact that many cultures believe that female circumcision (or genital mutilation, as campaigners against it believe is more accurate) is morally right does not mean that it really is. That people hold certain values doesn't show that they ought to do so. Similarly, if we discover that surreptitious male infidelity has evolved as a successful strategy for increasing the survival probabilities of his genes, that does not in itself show that it is morally right. Just because something is natural it doesn't automatically mean it is good, as people who go around eating wild mushrooms indiscriminately will soon find out to their cost.

So if you are to claim that a scientific fact tells us something about what we ought to do, then you need to provide a good reason for making that leap from *description* to *prescription*. And this is something that many who claim science tells us about morality fail to do. Take Sam Harris, for example. His argument is basically that 'Meaning, values, morality, and the good life must relate to facts about the well-being of conscious creatures – and, in our case, must lawfully depend on events in the world and the states of the human brain.'[68] If we grant this, then he claims that 'there must be a science of morality, whether or not we ever succeed in developing it'.[69]

There are at least three reasons why this is, at the very least, questionable. First of all, Harris acknowledges that the argument depends on us accepting that morality must 'relate to facts about the well-being of conscious creatures'. 'Relate to' is actually too weak a link for his purposes. What he really means is that matters of right and wrong are *determined* purely on the basis of how they contribute to or detract from well-being. This is certainly a credible hypothesis and clearly some moral theories, in particular consequentialist ones, endorse it. Harris even has an argument for it. But it is not a scientific one. And that should not be a surprise because it is not a *scientific* principle. You cannot establish that 'morality = well-being' is true in the same way that you can establish that force = mass x acceleration. But if the fundamental moral judgement that underpins everything else he says cannot be determined by science, then neither can morality as a whole.

Second, even if we allow that well-being is the basis for morality, 'well-being' is not a scientifically tractable term. Even if you can measure things like happiness, intensity of pleasure and pain and so on, those readings alone will not tell you whether or not a person is living a good life. The reason for that is simple: it is just not clear on the basis of evidence alone how much the good life depends on feeling good, judging one's own life to be worthwhile, doing good for others and so on. The components of well-being are controversial, and reasonable people can disagree about which are most important. If that's true, science cannot determine which of two people has more well-being or tell us what we need to do to maximize it.

The third problem for Harris perhaps explains why the whole project is misconceived. Harris's argument hinges on the fact that well-being 'must lawfully depend on events in the world and the states of the human brain'. This is surely true. We cannot have a single thought or feeling without something going on in our brains, which are embodied and situated in a physical world. But it doesn't follow from the fact that morality has a neural basis, that it can be determined on the basis of neurology. It's just the wrong level of description. Down at the level of neurons there is no right and there is no wrong. Like sensation, thought, appreciation, music and all the other riches of conscious life, morality may rest on nothing more than firing neurons. But it is an *emergent property* of those physical processes. That is to say, it appears only when the physical stuff is arranged and is working in the right way. Break it down to its constituent parts, however, and it disappears. And that means if you go looking for it under an electron microscope, it disappears too. Morality can only be seen, let alone understood, once you are at the scale of whole human beings, even if you accept that at bottom we are no more than arrangements of molecules, like everything else in the universe.

This is the same reason, by the way, why Rosenberg is also mistaken. His key idea is that 'the physical fact fix all the facts', meaning that, ultimately, 'all the processes in the universe, from, atomic to bodily to mental, are purely physical processes involving fermions and bosons interacting with each other'.[70] Again, this might well be true, but all it means is that morality doesn't come into the picture at the base level of description. That does not mean it is not real and does not emerge if fermions and bosons are arranged in the incredibly complicated and intricate way that is needed to give rise to creatures like us.

What science has to say

It would be wrong, however, to think that because people like Rosenberg and Harris claim too much for what science can tell us about morality that it has no useful contribution to make at all. There are scientists and philosophers of science who take a more modest view. One is Patricia Churchland, who works on the interface between neuroscience and philosophy. She rejects Harris's view but that does not mean she thinks neuroscience should butt out of ethics. Far from it.[71]

Churchland believes that moral problems are essentially 'constraint satisfaction problems', meaning they are about finding solutions to conflicts that emerge when people have to live together with limited resources. When it comes to finding such solutions, however, she says, 'I don't think neuroscience has anything to say about those things.' What it does have something to say about is the 'neural platform' on which these decision-making, solution-finding processes work. This neural platform is,

> the basis for sociality, it's the circuitry in place that makes us want to be with others, that makes us sacrifice sometimes our own interests because we want to be with others, and feel pain when we're excluded or when we're ostracized, enjoy the company of others, enjoy the feelings of satisfaction when we co-operate.[72]

But you can never determine what our moral values should be purely by understanding the platform because 'out of the platform then emerges very different social practices and they're influenced by many things', including history, culture and ecological conditions. Nevertheless, such work on the platform may well inform and enrich our moral understanding by helping us better understand how real moral thinking works. In short, Churchland believes moral reasoning is a somewhat mysterious way of finding solutions to constraint satisfaction problems and one which has very little to do with reasoning in logical steps by deduction. 'Who thinks deduction gets you around the planet,' she says. 'Really? I mean like maybe I do a deduction about twice a week.'

A similar need to understand the scientific basis of ethics while not reducing morality to science, or eliminating it altogether, is illustrated by the debate around evolution and morality. The general consensus that has emerged among evolutionary psychologists is that all the key elements of morality – a sense of fairness, willingness to co-operate, feelings of shame and guilt, a desire to punish cheats and so on – can be explained as emerging from the need for human beings to work together so as to maximize their individual chances of passing on their genes. Goodness and altruism are actually therefore simply means to the ends of selfish genes.

All this may well be true and I for one am confident that it is. But in thinking about what follows from this we have to be careful to avoid the 'genetic fallacy', which is to confuse truths about origins with truths about justification. A simple stark example is the science behind the link between smoking and lung cancer. It is widely believed that the first scientists to recognize this were the Nazi doctors of the Third Reich. But the conclusion is not invalidated by its Nazi origins. It stands or falls on the evidence for its truth, not where the evidence came from. The same distinction between origin and justification tells us that whatever we might discover about the origins of altruism and morality in the evolution of selfish genes, it does not necessarily tell us anything about what their justification is now.

One reason this is such an important point is that many people believe that what the origins of ethics tell us about the justification of morality is that it has none. Evolution *debunks* morality: it exposes what we think of as high principle as really involving nothing more than blind biological forces operating to ensure survival. Morality is a 'veneer' or 'illusion' that covers over a darker, atavistic reality. But it is far from a plain scientific truth that evolution does any such thing.

Janet Radcliffe Richards explains this point with admirable lucidity, distinguishing between reductive and debunking explanations. A reductive explanation 'explains a set of phenomena by reference to a more fundamental level of explanation and uses quite different terminology'.[73] Evolutionary psychology is reductive in this sense 'in explaining our mental and emotional attributes in terms of the survival value of genes'. This does not, however, mean we have to conclude our mental and emotional attributes are not real. 'It is an explanation at a different level,' says Radcliffe Richards, 'and to explain the evolutionary organs of generosity is not to show that the generosity is not real, any more than to explain that the water in a bottle is a collection of hydrogen and oxygen atoms is to show that it is not real water.'

A debunking explanation, in contrast, explains a set of phenomena by reference to a more fundamental level of explanation in such a way as to render the former description obsolete. Evolution is sometimes a debunking explanation. Most obviously, because it explains the appearance of apparent design in the universe, it actually undermines the rationale for believing that this design is real. What looks like design is actually natural selection acting on random mutation. Evolutionary explanations of morality would be debunking if, for example, they explained altruism in such a way as to 'allege a selfish motive underlying the apparently altruistic act'. But, says Radcliffe Richards, they do no such thing. They say nothing about our motives at all, because they are not considering our current motives but their evolutionary origins.

Informing yes, determining no

Clearly there is more to be said for and against Harris, Rosenberg, Churchland and Radcliffe Richards, as well as about other protagonists in this wide-ranging debate. But this brief sketch should make the terrain of the debate clear. The way Harris sets it up, it appears to be a disagreement between those who say facts have nothing to tell us about values and those who accept that science does reveal truths about how our minds work. If that were the way the battle lines were drawn, we'd have to be on the side of Harris et al. But the majority of those who want to severely limit what science can tell us about morality do not argue so because they are in denial of our physical nature or ideologically committed to maintaining an area of inquiry independent from science. Everyone should accept that facts can inform our values and that having false beliefs about the world can lead you to very bad ethics.

As Rosenberg points out about the Nazis, 'it was their wildly false *factual* beliefs about Jews, Roma, gays and Communist Commissars, combined with a moral core they shared with others, that led to the moral catastrophe of the Third Reich'.[74] Scientific facts about the non-existence of racial or gender superiority are vital in the case for equality. What those sceptical of handing morality over to science object to, is the failure to recognize the differences between debunking and reductive explanations, explaining and explaining away, origins and justifications, facts and values. This failure is a rational one, not a moral one, but it could have important moral consequences, especially if it leads people to become sceptical about the reality of morality.

Is morality relative?
The variability of moral codes

We live in a world in which individuality rules and in which the consumer is king. But if personal freedoms and preferences are of supreme importance and one-size-fits-all won't do, then shouldn't we accept that morality is as variable as taste in food or clothes? Can it not be that what's right for you is wrong for me? Or is this just the route to moral anarchy?

There are some people who have such traumatic, short lives that even those who believe that the universe is governed by a loving creator question their faith. One such child was Victoria Climbié. Born in Ivory Coast, she moved with her great-aunt Marie-Thérèse Kouao to be educated in Paris, and the two later moved on to Ealing, London. No one knows when, but at some point the relative to whom she had been entrusted started abusing her. The report into the circumstances of her death includes harrowing details of what the poor girl had to suffer. She was 'forced to sleep in the bath', 'tied up inside a black plastic sack in an effort to stop her from soiling the bath' and 'forced to eat by pushing her face towards the food, like a dog'. She was 'beaten on a regular basis' by both Kouao and her boyfriend Carl Manning, who testified that Kouao used to strike Victoria 'using a variety of weapons' including 'a shoe, a hammer, a coat hanger and a wooden cooking spoon'.[75] The final result of this was inevitable. As a later House of Commons Health Committee report coldly put it, 'Victoria Climbié died in the intensive care unit of St Mary's Hospital Paddington on 25 February 2000, aged 8 years and 3 months. Her death was caused by multiple injuries arising from months of ill-treatment and abuse.'[76]

Cases like this are sometimes used as a quick and apparently decisive response to people who claim that morality is relative: what is right for some people is wrong for others and vice versa. Yet surely everyone would agree Victoria Climbié was treated wrongly, full stop. The idea that it could be 'right for some' is grotesque. But that is not the main reason why Climbié's case is particularly relevant to the debate about relativism. What makes it an important example is that moral relativism may have contributed to her death.

Deep in Lord Laming's dense inquiry report lie some clues as to how this could be so. When the social worker Lisa Arthuworrey heard about Victoria 'standing to attention' before Kouao and Manning she 'concluded that this type of relationship was one that can be seen in many Afro-Caribbean families because respect and obedience are very important features of the Afro-Caribbean family script'.

Laming also records that 'Pastor Pascal Orome told me that he attributed Victoria's potentially concerning behaviour to the fact that she had come "freshly" from Africa.'

In both cases, Laming identified the key problem as being that people made false, unfounded assumptions about the way people did things in other cultures. But there is a deeper problem in the fact that 'cultural norms and models of behaviour can vary considerably between communities and even families'. That is, people often feel unable to condemn anything they see being done in another community for fear of appearing judgemental, imperialistic or plain racist. As Dr Mary Rossiter told the inquiry,

> *I was aware that as a white person I had to be sensitive to the feelings of people of all races and backgrounds, both clinically and with professionals. Maybe some social workers felt they knew more about black children than I did.*

It does not seem to be stretching the truth of this case to say that a widespread belief that people from one community are not qualified to judge the values of another may have contributed to the failure of authorities to be as alarmed as they should have been about certain evident facts about how Victoria was being treated.

That conclusion would shock many who assume that relativism is true and associate it with benign virtues such as tolerance, respect for diversity and individual choice. In contrast, it is assumed that a belief in moral absolutes – that some things just are wrong for everyone – is oppressive, arrogant and authoritarian.

On the other hand, there are also those who believe very strongly that relativism is the root of much modern evil, leaving people with no real values to guide them apart from their own selfish self-interest. Perhaps unsurprisingly, religious leaders are among the most vocal members of this camp. Pope Benedict XVI, for example, quoting St Paul's Letter to the Ephesians, has said that

> letting oneself be 'tossed here and there, carried about by every wind of doctrine', seems the only attitude that can cope with modern times. We are building a dictatorship of relativism that does not recognize anything as definitive and whose ultimate goal consists solely of one's own ego and desires.'[77]

He used the phrase 'dictatorship of relativism' again five years later, saying that it 'threatens to obscure the unchanging truth about man's nature, his destiny and his ultimate good'.[78]

Anything goes?

What, then, really is this relativism and is it permissive and dangerous or tolerant and benign? Relativism stands in opposition to absolutism. An absolutist conception of ethics holds that moral truths and principles hold for all people at all times, in all relevantly similar circumstances. For instance, if murder is wrong, then it is always wrong. It can't be permitted in order to achieve a greater good or because a murderer lives in a culture which glorifies homicide. Similarly, if female genital mutilation is wrong, it is always wrong, and the fact that some cultures practice it does not mean that it is right in their culture: it simply means their culture institutionalizes a morally wrong practice.

Absolutism seems to be required by the principle of universalisability, which maintains that it is of the nature of moral judgements that if we say an action is wrong in situation A, we must at the same time be saying that it would also be wrong in any other situation which resembles situation A in the morally relevant ways.

Relativism rejects this, claiming that 'What may be right for one person may not be right for another' and 'There is no objective way of determining right from wrong'. But it does not follow from this that 'anything goes'. For one thing, we need to remember that relativism comes in various forms. Morality might be relative to culture, the individual, historic epoch, species or circumstances. But to say it is relative doesn't necessarily mean it is relative to *everything*. For example, if we are cultural relativists, then it might be true that adultery is wrong in one culture and right in another, but that doesn't mean 'anything goes', because it *really* would be wrong in one culture and right in the other.

Consider as an analogy whether water is *really* solid, liquid or gas. The question is slightly absurd. The answer is relative to temperature and air pressure. In some states, water is a liquid, in others a solid and in others a gas. Yet we have no problem understanding that it *really is* each of these incompatible things in different circumstances. In the same way, it does not follow from the claim that a practice is right in one context and wrong in another that it is not *really* right or wrong in either.

'What may be right for one person may not be right for another' is therefore not an absurd claim that moral judgements have no force. But is it right? There are many reasons to believe that it often is. Imagine two different countries. In one, it is rude to shake hands with an elder, in the other it is rude not to do so. Furthermore, in one culture insulting someone is taken as a very serious moral failing, whereas in the other, insults are generally dished out and taken phlegmatically. Whether it is right or wrong to shake hands with an elder is therefore relative. What would be right for someone to do in one culture would be wrong in another. The difference is not just explained by appeal to a shared absolute principle – that insulting is wrong – because the cultures also differ as to how seriously insult is taken. Nor is this simply a matter of etiquette, because how you behave might seriously affect the mental well-being of others.

Take another example. Janet is confident, optimistic and has plenty of savings. Alice is timid, pessimistic, almost broke and has two children. They both work for the same company but in different departments, and the company needs to make one person redundant in each department. But the boss knows that, whereas Janet will cope and bounce back, Alice will be made miserable and broke by being laid off. For that reason, she decides that, although Janet and Alice are the worst performing staff member in their respective departments, she will only use performance as the deciding criterion for redundancy in Janet's department. Even if we do not agree with her conclusion, I think we would say that the boss is behaving very morally by trying to decide what is right relative to each individual.

I don't think it is difficult to come up with many other similar examples. Faced with such counter-examples, the absolutist has two options: either to deny that the two cases should be treated differently or to claim that absolutism allows for the differences. I think the first strategy is very unwise, since there are bound to be at least some cases in which 'one rule fits all' will turn out to be absurd. So what of the second? Can absolutism be made flexible enough to deal with the kind of variation according to circumstances a sophisticated morality needs?

Absolutely relative

One way of arguing that absolutism has the flexibility to deal with the different demands morality places on us in different situations is to claim that underpinning every apparent case of morality being relative is a more fundamental, absolute moral principle.

For example, could it not be that the absolute moral principle is 'act so as to cause the greatest happiness of the greatest number', as utilitarians believe? To follow that rule might mean shaking hands in one culture and not shaking hands in another; or laying off the least efficient person in one situation, but not in another. Or what about another possible candidate for the ultimate moral rule: 'do unto others as you would have done unto you'? How you would want to be treated might depend on what your culture's conventions are, or how well you'd be able to cope with hardship, so again, huge variation results in what is actually right or wrong.

This strategy has two problems. First of all, if it is right, it actually doesn't preserve the kind of absolutism many absolutists want, but it does allow the huge range of variation of moral rules that relativists defend. What it might therefore show is that relativism contains an element of absolutism after all, or that absolutism contains elements of relativism. Indeed, we might conclude that the terms 'relativist' and 'absolutist' are supremely unhelpful, since the true moral view combines elements of both.

But this solution may not work anyway. We have over two thousand years of striving to find the one moral principle that underpins all others and still we can't agree on what it is. The empirical evidence is therefore that no such principle exists. We can identify many things that matter for morality: happiness, respect, equality and so on. But it is impossible to say that one principle is the master principle, from which all other moral rules are derived. In different times, at different places, for different people, moral priorities change. Just as babies, children, adults and the elderly need to be treated differently, so other variations in the human condition require different moral responses. That, I suspect, is the truth that makes some kind of relativism inevitable.

Flexible absolutes

Absolutists may have another response to the apparent need for variation in moral rules. Remember that absolutism says that if something is wrong in one situation, it is also wrong in any other situation which is similar in all the morally relevant ways. The cases of handshaking, and of Alice and Janet, however, do differ in morally different ways. Therefore, isn't it consistent with absolutism to treat the cases differently?

This sounds convincing but hasn't the absolutist conceded too much? For if 'morally relevant differences' include facts about culture, individuals, circumstances and so on, isn't that just another way of saying that morality is relative to culture, individual or circumstance? Isn't relativism simply the acceptance that there are so many 'morally significant differences' between situations that trying to define 'absolute moral principles' is futile?

If the relativist is sounding surprisingly reasonable rather than anarchically mad, that's possibly because the relativist is usually only portrayed in his most grotesque, pantomime form. The version of relativism we are usually presented with is a cartoon caricature, of the person who simply shrugs his shoulders when faced with a moral dilemma, unwilling or unable to make any judgement. Such an absolute relativist has indeed left morality as we recognize it behind. The trouble is such cartoon relativists are rare. They are best described not as relativists, but moral sceptics.

Moral sceptics believe that no genuine moral judgements are possible. They can believe this for a variety of reasons. For instance, they may hold that there are no such things as moral facts, and if there are no facts about ethics, then you cannot say anything true or false about it. Alternatively, they might hold any number of 'veneer' theories, which argue that morality is just an attractive gloss we put upon the ugly reality that, for instance, what we consider good is simply what suits the powerful, what makes us feel better, or what we have evolved to believe. It should be clear that relativists need not be moral sceptics at all. They do believe that we can make moral judgements and that they mean something. It's just that they deny that it makes any sense to describe these judgements as absolute.

Religious relativism

A rather different reason people have for arguing that ethics is and needs to be absolute is that they think that ethics is, and must be, grounded in the divine. God sets the moral rules, and God's rules apply to all, irrespective of time and place. The problem here is that, actually, there are reasons to believe that God, if he exists, is the greatest relativist of them all.

Let's say, for example, that you are a Christian. In the Book of Leviticus, there are all sorts of bizarre-sounding rules, laid down by God, which Christians no longer feel themselves obliged to follow. These include the death penalty for homosexuals and children who do not respect their parents, bans on eating hares and calamari, prohibitions on men trimming their beards, and approval of slavery. Most Christians believe, however, that the New Testament supersedes the Old and that these rules no longer apply. What this adds up to is the belief that what was wrong for the ancient

Israelites is not wrong for modern Christians, on God's command. That seems to me like a clear combination of relativism and the belief that God's will underpins ethics.

In many ways this should not be surprising, since many have argued that the trouble with divine command theory – the idea that what is right or wrong is what God commands – is that it leaves open the possibility that God could command what is currently wrong to be right and vice versa. (See the next chapter for more on this.) Christian texts seem to provide evidence that this is precisely what their God has done.

There are many people who hold the view that God makes himself manifest to people in different ways, and so it's not the case that only one of the world's religions is right and the rest are wrong, but that all are right in their own ways. But again, since different religions make different moral demands of people, if many religions are true, God must be a relativist, for he requires different things from Jews, Hindus, Sikhs, Muslims, Christians and members of any other religion.

The strange thing is that I have often found religious people very sanguine about the idea that, as circumstances change, God might require different things from different people in different places at different times. But these same people are horrified by the idea of relativism, as the pope's homilies exemplify.

One size doesn't fit all

Far from leaving us without the possibility of morality, there is a serious case for a kind of relativism that takes moral judgement seriously and does not inevitably lead to laissez-faire permissiveness. This, however, is not the kind of relativism that has crept into general culture and which people like the Pope lambast. This 'lazy relativism' ends its thinking where it should only really begin: with an acceptance of the variability of moral judgements. What the case of Victoria Climbié shows is the danger of this simplistic kind of relativism, which suspends judgement in the name of tolerance and pluralism. A more demanding relativism is possible.

That is not to say, of course, that moral relativism is correct. That case has not here been made. But even if ultimately we reject relativism, the lesson is that it is possible and surely sometimes necessary to accept that what is right and wrong can vary significantly with circumstances, and we should not fear any moral position that allows for that.[79]

Without God, is everything permitted?

The link between morality and religion

Like many other of the most famous 'quotes' of all time, the person to whom 'Without God, everything is permitted' is attributed didn't quite say it. Never mind: it expresses the idea expressed by Mitya Karamazov in one of Dostoevsky's The Brothers Karamazov much better than the original. More importantly, it perfectly encapsulates a persuasive and widespread idea: no God, no morality.

In our world of people of many faiths and none, we rarely accuse people with different world views of lacking any morality. Atheists are the exception to this rule. The current pope, for instance, has more than once suggested that if morality is not God-given then it cannot have any other source, certainly not a human one. In his second encyclical, he wrote 'the claim that humanity can and must do what no God actually does or is able to do is both presumptuous and intrinsically false'. Not only false, but dangerous: 'It is no accident that this idea has led to the greatest forms of cruelty and violations of justice; rather, it is grounded in the intrinsic falsity of the claim', since 'only God can create justice'.[80]

He returned to this theme a few years later during his state visit to the United Kingdom. In the presence of the Queen, he said,

> As we reflect on the sobering lessons of the atheist extremism of the 20th century, let us never forget how the exclusion of God, religion and virtue from public life leads ultimately to a truncated vision of man and of society and thus to a 'reductive vision of the person and his destiny'.

What made these remarks even more pointed were that they came in the same paragraph as a remark about 'a Nazi tyranny that wished to eradicate God from society'.[81]

Atheists are in turns bemused and angered by such comments. They see the idea that the godless are inherently amoral or immoral as being one of the great distorting misconceptions of our age. No wonder that atheist organizations have often made a point of their positive moral values in their advertising campaigns. The American Humanist Association, for instance, used the slogan 'Be good for goodness' sake', as opposed to being good for the sake of a God who might just punish you if you are not good. The Humanist Society of Scotland similarly came up with the slogan 'Good without God'.

The contradictory assertions on both sides are clear enough. So who is right? Can there be morality without God?

An ancient dilemma

Whenever this issue is discussed, there's no avoiding the fact that the original, and arguably still best, treatment of it is in Plato's dialogue *Euthyphro*. The protagonist, Socrates, poses a simple dilemma: 'whether the pious or holy is beloved by the gods because it is holy, or holy because it is beloved of the gods'. Plato lived in a time of many gods. To make this more clearly relevant to the contemporary debate it's helpful to substitute 'good' for 'pious' and 'God' for 'gods'. We could also think of what God commands rather than what he loves. The question then becomes: does God command what is good because it is good, or are things only good because God commands them?

The second option describes what is known as divine command theory: that actions are made right or wrong only by God's decree, they are not right or wrong in themselves. There is a clear exposition of this thesis in the writings of the medieval philosopher William of Ockham, who wrote of acts such as 'hatred, theft, adultery, and the like' that

> *God can perform them without involving any evil. And they*
> *can even be performed meritoriously by someone on earth if*

they should fall under a divine command, just as now the
opposite of these, in fact, fall under a divine command.[82]

This strikes many as a bizarre and troubling thought. The
idea that God could just decree that all that we thought evil
was in fact good and vice versa seems to make a mockery of
the seriousness of ethics. It makes right and wrong ultimately arbitrary. That surely can't be right? Think of the
most evil acts, such as sadistic torture. How could they ever
be made good simply by God deciding they are?

We must then surely reject the option that things are
good only because God commands them and instead opt
for the other possibility: that God commands what is good
because it is good. But if this is true, then it is clear that
goodness is a property that things have independently of
God's will. God's commanding something does not make it
good. Rather, it is already good and that is why God
commands it. Yet that seems compatible with a truly moral
God, one who wants us to do things because they are good,
rather than a megalomaniac for whom wanting us to do
something is a good enough reason in and of itself to
demand we do it. God is often described as our 'father' but
he is surely not the tyrannical kind who thinks 'because I
said so' is a good enough reason to obey him.

In philosophy, knock-down arguments are rare, perhaps
even non-existent. But many believe Plato's *Euthyphro*

dilemma is as close as philosophy can get to settling an issue once and for all. That is not to say there aren't people who claim that divine command theory can get back up on its feet, recover and win. One way it is claimed it can do this is by arguing that, because goodness is essentially a property of God and is not independent of him, the dilemma is falsely posed. Something is good because God commands it, but what God commands is not arbitrary since he *is* goodness itself.

This doesn't seem to work, however, because the dilemma can just be restated: is God's nature good because it is good or good because it's God's? To insist that you can't ask this question because God and good can't be separated seems to dodge the issue. The very idea of a mountain, for example, implies the idea of great height. So you can't have a mountain that isn't high. But the concept of height is separable from the concept of mountain in that it can apply to other things too. So you can ask: is being a mountain what makes a landmass high, or is it being high that makes a landmass a mountain? The answer is the latter: a mountain is a mountain in virtue of being high; height is not defined by whatever a mountain is. By the same logic, even if God is by definition good, we can still ask if it is through being good that God is by definition good, or whether it is by being a property of God that good is defined as it is.

It follows that the claim that the idea of goodness requires an idea of God seems to be false. Indeed, the good must be comprehensible independently of the idea of God, otherwise it loses all its moral force. The good cannot be simply what God commands and so it must be something else. But what?

Where goodness lies

The Euthyphro dilemma is usually taken to show something important about the independence of ethics from God. But some would argue it shows something more: the independence of ethics from *anyone*. The idea is simple. Ethics must be independent of God's will or else it becomes arbitrary. But if it is independent of God then surely it must in some sense have an objective truth of its own.

Forget about God for a moment and just think about good people. Let's call it the Anthropro dilemma, the dilemma as it is for (pro) humans (anthro): do good people choose actions because they are right, or are actions right because good people choose them? The second possibility sounds even more absurd than the idea that actions are right just because God commands them. The answer is surely that good people choose actions because they are right. But that would seem to mean that the truth of moral statements is independent of human choice and action. And that implies that morality is objective.

There is, however, a hypothetical element to this argument. All this shows is that if there are such things as good people, then morality has to be objective and independent of human choice. So, rather than proving that morality is objective, the dilemma now becomes one about which way we jump on one of the most fundamental debates about the nature of morality: either there really are good people and right choices, in which case morality is objective; or else morality is not objective but is the product of arbitrary choices of human beings. And that would suggest that if objective ethics does not exist, then everything is permitted.

The Euthyphro dilemma has now metamorphozed into something to trouble secular as well as religious thinkers. Many atheistic moral philosophers have been convinced that morality is *not* objective. Indeed, they find it hard to even imagine what this would mean. In what possible sense can moral values have an independent, objective existence? There are no 'oughts' or 'musts' in the laws of physics. In a naturalistic universe, there is no celestial place where rules are engraved on tablets of stone. In short, moral principles seem to be the wrong kinds of things to have an independent, objective existence.

Nevertheless, most who reject the idea of an objective morality still believe that ethics is real and has some claim on us. How can this be so? There are many answers, but in general it is because morality does not have a single foundation. Rather it emerges out of the confluence of certain facts, desires, feelings and needs. The *facts* include that pain is unpleasant, people want to avoid it and animals feel it too; or that there are no morally significant differences between people with different skin colours; or that how wealthy or talented a person is has a lot to do with chance. The *desires* include the wish to live life free from illusion, not to be hypocritical or to be appreciated for good reasons. The *feelings* include empathetic distress at the suffering of others and pleasure in making others feel better. And the *needs* include the necessity of living in peace with each other, being able to trust them and to co-operate.

If you put all these things together, you can see quite readily how something like morality emerges. Given brute facts and our desires, feelings and needs, we have good reason to uphold justice, to be fair and honest in our dealings with people, to show compassion, not to kill the innocent, and so on. These four factors together add up to a rationale for morality that is more than just enlightened self-interest, although that too is part of the mix and more often than not doing the right thing is better for us than not doing the right thing, in the long run at least.

This does not, however, seem to add up to an 'objective' morality. It has objective components, in that objective facts play a role, as do needs that we have simply in virtue of being human. But because it also involves feelings and desires, it falls short of proving a fully objective basis for ethics. If someone says, for instance, that they just don't want to get on with their fellow humans or don't care about suffering, there is no way of showing them objectively that they must desire otherwise or that their feelings are defective.

Given that, it should now be obvious that the Anthropro dilemma is based on what is either a false or at least a misleading dichotomy: a choice between an objective morality and a purely arbitrary one. To say a choice is arbitrary means it is based on personal whim or preference, without constraint. It could just as easily have been completely different. Now in what sense is the kind of morality that emerges out of facts, desires, feelings and needs arbitrary? Only in the sense that there is no external power or principle that forces us to choose the values we do. If we really wanted to decree that 'hatred, theft, adultery, and the like' were morally permissible, then like Euthyphro's God, we could do so if we wanted. In *that* sense ethics is arbitrary and without God, everything is permitted.

But that is not how most of us would understand 'arbitrary'. Our morality is not capricious but is based on certain facts about human nature and our need to get on, along with desires and feelings that maintain their validity when scrutinized even though they lack the solidity of plain facts. So if we think about whether it is right to love, for instance, there is no objective, rationally compelling argument for saying that it is. Nonetheless, we can see the benefits that love provides, as well as its drawbacks, and can see that there are good reasons why people should want it and no good reason why someone should want to destroy it. Someone who sets out to deprive others of love is therefore not guilty of a logical mistake, but there are good reasons why we would be right to try to thwart him. And because we do indeed follow such rules and uphold them through law and social pressure, even without God, many things are not permitted.

This may appear fairly easy to see and understand, yet many continue to believe that unless ethics has a fully objective basis, it must be subjective. The mistake, I think, lies in seeing the categories of subjective and objective as pairs of an either/or choice. It is both more truthful and helpful to see it in terms explained by Thomas Nagel in *The View from Nowhere*. For Nagel, objectivity is not absolute but a matter of degree. Our viewpoint is more objective the less it depends on 'the specifics of the individual's makeup and position in the world'.[83] It is difficult, perhaps impossible, to make sense of objectivity in any other way, because there simply is no way for humans to gain knowledge which is completely independent of our own makeup and position in the universe.

Understood in this way, you can see how it is possible to have a morality that is more subjective than, say, molecular biology, but more objective than taste in music. The fear of subjectivity in ethics is therefore overstated. There is no problem if there is a subjective component in moral thinking – how could it be otherwise? It's only a problem if we let the subjective element dominate too much, leaving things to the caprice of individuals or the historical accidents of current social practices.

If all this provides a way out of the Anthropro dilemma, can it do the same for the Euthyphro dilemma? Yes and no. If God were not constrained by objective morality, he would be no more likely to choose arbitrarily then we would. Like us, there would be nothing to stop him inverting all moral values, but he would have good reasons not to do so. God would not make his choices randomly, but on the basis of facts, desires, feelings and needs.

But the critical point of the Euthyphro would still hold: we don't need God to figure out what is right and wrong. That is not to say God wouldn't make a difference to morality. First of all, there is sense in which the existence of a certain kind of God would make certain things impermissible in the sense that people would be punished if they did them. But this isn't usually what is meant by 'permitted'. Without an effective police force, it's not that *everything is permitted* but *nothing is enforced*.

Second, if there were a God then we would have every reason to think he would be a better judge of what is right than us. So, if we also believed we had access to his guidance, we would be justified in following it. Nonetheless, given the ambiguity of most religious texts and the huge disagreements about what exactly God does want us to do, in practice this is a small loss. We can't know for sure what God thinks is best for us so we have to fall back on our own judgement in any case.

So there are losses for morality if there is no God, in that we have no guarantee that justice will ultimately be upheld and we can't rely on religious teachings as some kind of imperfect, but perhaps helpful, guide to how to live. Nonetheless, to say there are losses for morality is not to say morality is lost. We can indeed be good without God, for goodness' sake. And, as I hope this book has illustrated, we can be helped along the way by the rich resource of moral philosophy.

Can all moral dilemmas be resolved?

The limits of ethics

In morality, as in many other difficult areas of life, we want answers, so much so that we'll often prefer a clear answer with a weak justification than accept a good justification for why there is no clear answer. Accepting a lack of answers in ethics is particularly difficult, since it seems to most of us that surely there must be some way of knowing what the right thing to do is. But is there?

At the very end of Joseph Conrad's *Heart of Darkness*, the protagonist, Marlow, meets the bereaved fiancée of Kurtz, the man who had descended into savagery in the jungle and whose last words had been 'The horror! The horror!' She struck Marlow as someone who 'had a mature capacity for fidelity, for belief, for suffering'. Yet when she discovered Marlow was with Kurtz when he died and had heard his last words, she implored, 'Repeat them. I want – I want – something – something – to – to live with.' He was silent, remembering the words Kurtz had said as though 'the dusk was repeating them in a persistent whisper all around us, in a whisper that seemed to swell menacingly like the first whisper of a rising wind'.

'His last word – to live with,' she murmured. 'Don't you understand I loved him—I loved him – I loved him!'

What was the right thing to do? Tell the undiscoverable lie that would give her 'something to live with' or reveal the truth, and leave her to deal with it, even if it destroys her comforting illusions?

Here's a very different dilemma. Joe Simpson and Simon Yates's disastrous 1985 assent of the 6,344-metre Siula Grande in the Peruvian Andes has been immortalized in Simpson's brilliant book *Touching the Void* and an equally gripping film of the same name. The pivotal episode of the book comes when Simpson, who had already broken his leg, was being lowered by a 300-foot rope off the north ridge of the mountain. This too went wrong, as Simpson was left dangling off a cliff edge. Yates was holding the rope but he couldn't pull Simpson back up, and with his broken leg and frost-bitten hands, Simpson couldn't climb up himself. Dangling on the rope, Simpson gave up shouting to Yates, whom he realized would either 'die in his seat or be pulled from it by the constant strain of my body'.

On the ridge, Yates recalls thinking 'The knife! The thought came out of nowhere. Of course, the knife. Be quick and get on with it.'[84] Would this be the right thing to do? Cut the rope and condemn his climbing partner to death?

These two moral dilemmas are very different in many ways. What they have in common is that the choices on offer are incredibly difficult. But is that because there is no easy answer to either, or that there just is no answer at all. In other words, are some moral dilemmas not just difficult but unresolvable?

There must be an answer

In order for any moral dilemma to be capable of resolution, two things must be in place. The first is that moral principles have to have some kind of objectivity. 'Some kind' is deliberately vague because it may not be necessary that they are objective in the most complete sense: that is, in having a real existence independently of human thought and culture. All that is required is that there is an agreed standard for distinguishing real differences between moral principles that are valid and those that are not. If there are no such differences, then moral dilemmas can have no correct resolution because there will be no yardstick against which to measure whether one choice is better than another.

This objectivity, however, is not enough by itself to enable all moral dilemmas to be resolved. What must also be true is that moral principles must be rankable in some kind of hierarchy, so that it is always possible to decide which principle trumps if they conflict. For example, in the *Heart of*

Darkness case, there is a conflict between compassion and truth. It may be that both are objectively good, but unless there is some fact of the matter as to which takes precedence over the other, simply recognizing this objectivity cannot resolve the dilemma. In the *Touching the Void* case, the principles in tension are between the need to do what is most likely to serve the welfare of all involved and the duty to do all you can to protect the life of a friend, someone whose fate you have (in this case literally) tied to your own by embarking on a dangerous adventure together.

We might be able to get by with less than full objectivity here because, in practice, all we need to construct such a hierarchy is what is sometimes called 'inter-subjective' agreement. If, for example, we all agree that the right to life trumps the right to protect property from theft, then it is clear that someone faced with a choice between letting a burglar get away or stopping him with a bullet would be right to take the first option and wrong to take the second. We might well ask, in a philosophical mood, 'yes but are these principles objective? But that is simply an interesting theoretical aside. The dilemma is resolved whether or not we think the hierarchy is based on objective or inter-subjective principles. Inter-subjectivity can thus be thought of as 'some kind of objectivity' because it provides a basis for moral judgements that transcends the preferences of individuals or sub-groups, without reaching the heights of full independence from human belief.

Worries about the objectivity of moral values are not then necessarily a serious problem for constructing the hierarchy of values needed to resolve all dilemmas. But there are plenty of others. First of all, there is a problem of the degree of specificity needed to undertake such a ranking. Take, for instance, the values of truth and compassion. Surely hardly anyone who thought both were important would believe that one *always* trumped the other. So much depends on the particular situation and how salient each of these elements is. For example, you wouldn't conceal a very important truth in order to save someone a little discomfort, and it would be spiteful to reveal a trivial truth that would nonetheless cause a lot of distress.

That means you just can't arrange moral principles of any generality into a hierarchy of importance. You would at the very least need to break each principle down according to the seriousness of the kinds of cases each applies to. But grouping each kind of wrongdoing into categories with a certain negative value attached looks both impossible and misguided. You cannot attach values to types of action and then run each particular case though a moral algorithm to work out which is more serious. Even if different kinds of actions had objectively different levels of moral seriousness, ranking them according to type would require a certain amount of approximation, making any calculations based on them inaccurate. The only truly objective ranking would rate each action individually. So, rather than their being a hierarchy of moral principles, there would be a league table of all actions with a moral dimension.

There are two key problems with this theory. The first is the problem of *how we could ever know* where on such a table two actions we want to compare lie. To believe there is a fact of the matter but that one can't possibly know what it is leaves you in the same boat as someone who just believes there is no fact of the matter to be known. It may make some difference to your moral outlook, or in an academic context, when one is really trying to make sense of what morality is and how it works. But when we are concerned with moral philosophy as a tool of practical wisdom, such theoretical differences don't matter at all. When it comes to resolving a dilemma, you would be left having to rely on judgements rather than the mechanical application of rules.

However, many would say that the problem is not simply that we cannot know the rankings, but that *no such ranking is even theoretically possible*. If your view on ethics is anything other than that moral truths exist as objective absolutes, it is hard to see how morality could generate judgements with this degree of precision. You just cannot take this kind of actuarial approach to morality.

The most radical challenge to the notion of a hierarchy of wrongdoing, however, comes from moral pluralism. Isaiah Berlin, offered a very clear and compelling defence of what pluralism really is in an essay he wrote shortly before his death.[85] The central claim is almost banal in its obviousness: that 'there is a plurality of values which men can and do seek, and that these values differ'. So, for example, some may value solitary contemplation, others sociability. Some value ascetic restraint, others a hedonistic pursuit of pleasure.

So far, so good – but so what? People value different things, but that doesn't tell us anything about what they ought to value or what is right. What explains pluralism and differentiates it from relativism is how these differences in values are understood. Berlin says, 'I think these values are objective – that is to say, their nature, the pursuit of them, is part of what it is to be a human being, and this is an objective given.' The objectivity arises because 'the number of human values, of values that I can pursue while maintaining my human semblance, my human character, is finite'.

The key point here is that to say people value different things is not to say that anything can be of real objective value. It is not a legitimate human preference to value the extermination of ethnic groups or the subjugation of women, for example. Hence Berlin says,

I do not say 'I like my coffee with milk and you like it without;
I am in favour of kindness and you prefer concentration
camps' – each of us with his own values, which cannot be
overcome or integrated. This I believe to be false . . . that is
why pluralism is not relativism – the multiple values are
objective, part of the essence of humanity rather than arbi-
trary creations of men's subjective fancies.

Given there is such a plurality, it becomes clear, as Berlin
put it in another essay 'that values can clash – that is why
civilizations are incompatible'. But not just between civilizations. 'Values may easily clash within the breast of a single
individual; and it does not follow that, if they do, some must
be true and others false.' And this means that the hope of an
objective hierarchy of values that will enable us to resolve all
moral dilemmas is a false one.

These collisions of values are of the essence of what they are
and what we are. If we are told that these contradictions
will be solved in some perfect world in which all good things
can be harmonized in principle, then we must answer, to
those who say this, that the meanings they attach to the
names, which for us denote the conflicting values, are not
ours.[86]

Berlin makes a convincing case for the coherence of this
view. But what reasons do we have for thinking this is the

right one? Here we have one of those cases where I think we do not arrive at a conclusion by constructing an argument but by carefully attending to the relevant features of reality. And, for me, the clearest example that enables us to do this is to consider the comparative value of individualism and community. We know that there are good things about living in a close community, but also downsides, in terms of conformity, for instance. Similarly, individualism has its advantages but also its price, in terms of the loss of community support. Given that people are temperamentally different and both individuals and cultures have different needs at different times, can we really say that one value is simply superior to the others? I think we only need to observe human nature to see that this is not so. Individualism and community are two real values that pull in different directions and it is simply not the case that one is objectively superior to the other.

This might seem a pessimistic view, since it condemns us to live with incompatible values. But far from being an inevitable source of conflict, Berlin believes that pluralism offers the possibility of peaceful co-existence between people with different values. The reason it can do this is because all legitimate values are rooted in human nature, and this is shared. 'If I am a man or a woman with sufficient imagination (and this I do need), I can enter into a value system which is not my own, but which is nevertheless something I can conceive of men pursuing while remaining human, while remaining

246 WITHOUT GOD, IS EVERYTHING PERMITTED?

creatures with whom I can communicate, with whom I have some common values.'[87] Hence, for the same reason that not all moral dilemmas can be resolved, all reasonable moral differences can still be understood and so in some way lived with.

The final choice

So how did Conrad's Marlow and Simpson's climbing partner Simon Yates resolve their dilemmas? Yates was tied by a rope to Simpson, who was dangling above a crevice. If he cut it, Simpson would fall to almost certain death. If he didn't, in time he would be pulled over and they would both be killed. Yates recalled, 'I reached down again, and this time I touched the blade to the rope. It needed no pressure. The taut rope exploded at the touch of the blade.'

The dilemma hinged on competing values, those of doing the best for all concerned and sticking by a friend. But in this case it seems there was, if not an objective, at least an inter-subjective solution. Awful though the choice was, Yates was right to cut the rope. Simpson, who incredibly did survive, has always accepted that Yates did the right thing. Even as he hung by the rope he thought 'he shouldn't have to die for me'.

This incredible case illustrates how dilemmas can be acute, they can arise from a genuine clash of values, and there may be no objective fact about which value should prevail, but that nonetheless there are better or worse resolutions. But what about Marlow's dilemma in *Heart of Darkness*? Marlow had to decide whether to reveal Kurtz's true last words – 'The horror! The horror! – to his fiancé, or give her 'something to live with'. Eventually Marlow says, 'The last word he pronounced was – your name.'

'I knew it – I was sure!' she replied, weeping. Marlow couldn't bring himself to tell her the truth – 'It would have been too dark – too dark altogether' – even though the lie at first appeared to be an affront against reality. 'It seemed to me that the house would collapse before I could escape, that the heavens would fall upon my head. But nothing happened. The heavens do not fall for such a trifle.'

Was Marlow right? I don't think there is any way to establish this. There is no law of the universe that settles things, which is one reason why the heavens did not fall on Marlow's head. But still, we can give good reasons on either side and we may believe that one set really does outweigh the other. The lack of an objectively right solution to a dilemma is not a reason to give up thinking about it. Indeed, it might be a reason to think more. If Berlin is right and that pluralism lies at the root of many resolvable conflicts of values, then dilemmas are actually useful for getting us to attend to precisely which values we most want to assert and live by.

Together, these two dilemmas capture much of what is important about ethics. If we are looking for clear answers, strict objective rules, then I think we'll look in vain. If we think that all moral dilemmas can be resolved, we will be disappointed. But if we accept that we can make better moral choices, ones with genuinely better outcomes, by thinking clearly and attending carefully to what we really value, then there is a point to philosophical ethics. The final choice is always your own, and only you can bear responsibility for it. And to take that responsibility requires, I think, giving ethics the serious time and thought it deserves.

Endnotes

Preface

1 Lydia Saad, 'Fewer Americans Down on US Moral Values', Gallup.com, 25 May 2011, available at www.gallup.com/poll/147794/Fewer-Americans-Down-Moral-Values.aspx.

2 BBC Press release, 7 September 2007, available at www.bbc.co.uk/pressoffice/pressreleases/stories/2007/09_september/07/questions.shtml.

Is there a Golden Rule?

3 Immanuel Kant, *Groundwork of the Metaphysics of Morals*, Section 1, 4:402, trans. Mary Gregor (Cambridge University Press, 1998), p. 14.

4 John Searle, *Rationality in Action* (The MIT Press, 2001), pp. 158–61.

5 For a fuller version of my arguments see Julian Baggini, 'Morality as a Rational Requirement', *Philosophy*, vol. 77, no. 301, July 2002, pp. 447–53.

Do the Ends Justify the Means?

6 Fox News, 4 September 2011.

7 Robert P. Newman, *Truman and the Hiroshima Cult* (Michigan State University Press, 1995).

8 See www.bbc.co.uk/history/worldwars/wwtwo/nuclear_01.shtml.

Is Terrorism Ever Justified?

9 Ted Honderich, *After the Terror* (Edinburgh University Press, 2003), p. 151.

10 For Honderich's account of the Oxfam incident, see www.ucl.ac.uk/~uctytho/ATTOxfam1.html.

11 Jeremy Bentham, *A Fragment on Government* (1776), preface.

12 Ted Honderich, *Humanity, Terrorism, Terrorist War* (Continuum, 2006), p. 60.

13 J.S. Mill, *Utilitarianism* (1863), chapter 2.

14 Ted Honderich, 'Terrorism for Humanity', revised lecture transcript (2004), available at www.ucl.ac.uk/~uctytho/terrforhum.html.

Should We Favour Our Families and Friends?

15 Attributed to J. S. Mill in *Utilitarianism* (1863), chapter 5.
16 Adam Smith, *The Theory of Moral Sentiments*, Part 1 (1759).

How Much Should We Give to Charity?

17 Tom Geoghegan, 'Toby Ord: Why I'm giving £1m to charity', *BBC News Magazine*, 13 December 2010, available at www.bbc.co.uk/news/magazine-11950843.
18 Susanna Rustin, 'The Saturday Interview: Toby Ord and Bernadette Young on the joy of giving', *Guardian*, 24 December 2011.
19 Onora O'Neill, 'Lifeboat Earth', republished in *World Hunger and Moral Obligation*, ed. Aiken and LaFollette (Prentice-Hall, 1977).
20 Peter Singer, 'Famine, Affluence, and Morality', in *Philosophy and Public Affairs*, vol. 1, no. 1 (Spring 1972), pp. 229–43.
21 Peter Singer, 'The Life You Can Save'.
22 See www.lv.com/adviser/working-with-lv/news_detail?articleid=2183108.
23 See Julian Baggini, 'Out of Sight, out of Mind', *Independent*, 3 May 2010.

Are Drug Laws Morally Inconsistent?

24 David J. Nutt, 'Equasy: An Overlooked Addiction with Implications for the Current Debate on Drug Harms', *Journal of Psychopharmacology* 23 (2009), p. 3.
25 David J. Nutt, Leslie A. King and Lawrence D. Phillips, 'Drug Harms in the UK: A Multicriteria Decision Analysis', *The Lancet*, vol. 376, no. 9752 (2010), pp. 1558–65.

Do Animals Have Rights?

26 Peter Singer, *The Expanding Circle: Ethics, Evolution, and Moral Progress*, new edition (Princeton University Press, 2011).
27 Jeremy Bentham, 'Anarchical Fallacies; Being an Examination of the Declarations of Rights Issued During the French Revolution', *The Works of Jeremy Bentham*, vol. 2 (1843).
28 Jeremy Bentham, *An Introduction to the Principles of Morals and Legislation* (1789), chapter 17, footnote.
29 Daniel Kahneman, *Thinking Fast and Slow* (Allen Lane, 2011), pp. 379–80.

Is Abortion Murder?

30 Exodus 20:13.
31 Derek E. Wildman, Monica Uddin, Guozhen Liu, Lawrence I. Grossman and Morris Goodman, 'Implications of Natural Selection in Shaping 99.4 per cent Nonsynonymous DNA Identity between Humans and Chimpanzees: Enlarging Genus Homo', *Proceedings of the National Academy of Sciences*, vol. 100, no. 12, June 2003, pp. 7181–8.
32 Department of Health & Social Security, *Report of the Committee of Inquiry into Human Fertilization and Embryology*, chair Mary Warnock (Her Majesty's Stationery Office, 1984).
33 Job 1:21.

Should Euthanasia Be Legal?

34 BBC News, 12 May 2002, http://news.bbc.co.uk/1/hi/health/1983457.stm.
35 'Judgments – The Queen on the Application of Mrs Diane Pretty (Appellant) v Director of Public Prosecutions (Respondent) and Secretary of State for the Home Department (Interested Party)', House of Lords, 29 November 2001 (UKHL 61).
36 Boswell, *Life of Johnson* (Oxford University Press, 1970), pp. 496 and 735.

Is Sex a Moral Issue?

37 Peter Singer, *Practical Ethics*, second edition (Cambridge University Press, 1993), p. 2.
38 See Friedrich Nietzsche, *Beyond Good and Evil* (1886) and *On the Genealogy of Morals* (1887).

Can Discrimination Be Good?

39 John Stuart Mill, 'The Subjection of Women', 1869, http://feminism.eserver.org/history/docs/subjection-of-women.txt.

Is Free Trade Fair Trade?

40 Nick Gillespie, 'Poor Man's Hero', *Reason* (December 2003).
41 National Center for Policy Analysis, Month In Review, Trade June, 1996.
42 Lucy Martinez-Mont, 'Sweatshops Are Better than No Shops', *Wall Street Journal*, 25 June 1996.

Should We Protect the Environment?

43 For example, Fairfield Osborn, *Our Plundered Planet* (Little, Brown & Co., 1948); Edward Rogers, *Plundered Planet* (NCEC, 1974); Paul Collier, *The Plundered Planet* (Oxford University Press, 2010).
44 Deuteronomy 11:14–17.
45 Homer, *The Odyssey*, trans. Andrew Lang, with S.H. Butcher (P.F. Collier & Son, 1909–14), Book XI.
46 Prince Charles, Speech on 6 February 2003, www.princeofwales.gov.uk/speechesandarticles.
47 Richard Feynman, 'Personal Observations on Reliability of Shuttle', in *Report of the Presidential Commission on the Space Shuttle Challenger Accident* (NASA, 1986), vol. 2, appendix F.
48 *Climate Change 2007: Synthesis Report*, Intergovernmental Panel on Climate Change, www.ipcc.ch/publications_and_data/ar4/syr/en/contents.html.
49 John Beddington, 'Global Food System Faces challenges', *Bite* 6, 2011.
50 *Foresight: The Future of Food and Farming*. Final Project Report (The Government Office for Science, 2011), p. 92.

Are We Responsible for Our Actions?

51 Sorcha Griffith, 'Judge Rejects Mother's Plea That Her Son Had "No Control"', *Irish Independent*, 19 June 2007.
52 Plato, *Meno*, §77, trans. Benjamin Jowett.

What is a Just War?

53 Thomas Aquinas, *Summa Theologicæ, Second Part of the Second Part, Treatise on The Theological Virtues Question. 40: Of War* (1265–74).
54 Commons Hansard Debates, vol. 401, part 365, text for Tuesday, 18 March 2003.
55 See www.iraqbodycount.org.

Is Torture Always Wrong?

56 Eliza Manningham-Buller, 'The Reith Lectures 2: Security', BBC Radio Four, 13 September 2011, available at www.bbc.co.uk/programmes/b014fcyw.
57 Ali Soufan, 'My Tortured Decision', *New York Times*, 22 April 2009.
58 Immanuel Kant, *Groundwork of the Metaphysics of Morals*, trans. Mary Gregor (Cambridge University Press, 1998), Section 2, 4:4430, p. 38.
59 Bernard Williams, 'Utilitarianism and Moral Self Indulgence', in *Moral Luck* (Cambridge University Press, 1981), pp. 40–53.

What Can Science Tell Us about Morality?

60 Sam Harris, *The Moral Landscape: How Science Determines Human Values* (Bantam Press, 2010), p. 4.

61 Michael Ruse, 'Evolutionary Ethics – Part V', *Chronicle of Higher Education Brainstorm Blog*, 28 September 2011, http://chronicle.com/blogs/brainstorm/evolutionary-ethics-part-v.

62 Michael Ruse, 'Evolutionary Ethics – Part IV', *Chronicle of Higher Education Brainstorm Blog*, 15 August 2011, http://chronicle.com/blogs/brainstorm/evolutionary-ethics-part-iv.

63 Alex Rosenberg, *The Atheist's Guide to Reality* (W.W. Norton, 2011), pp. 97–8.

64 Stephen Jay Gould, *Rock of Ages: Science and Religion in Fullness of Life* (Vintage, 2002), p. 66.

65 Stephen Jay Gould, *Rock of Ages: Science and Religion in Fullness of Life* (Vintage, 2002), p. 6.

66 John Polkinghorne and Nicholas Beale, *Questions of Truth* (Westminster John Knox Press, 2009), p. 7.

67 David Hume, *A Treatise of Human Nature* (1739), Book III, part I, section I.

68 Sam Harris, *The Moral Landscape: How Science Determines Human Values* (Bantam Press, 2010), p. 6.

69 Sam Harris, *The Moral Landscape: How Science Determines Human Values* (Bantam Press, 2010), p. 28.

70 Alex Rosenberg, *The Atheist's Guide to Reality* (W.W. Norton, 2011), pp. 20–1.

71 Patricia Churchland, *Braintrust: What Neuroscience Tells Us about Morality* (Princeton University Press, 2011).

72 Julian Baggini, 'Interview with Patricia Churchland', *The Philosophers' Magazine*, 57/2 (2012).

73 Janet Radcliffe Richards, *Human Nature after Darwin* (Routledge, 2000), pp. 179–80.

74 Alex Rosenberg, *The Atheist's Guide to Reality* (W.W. Norton, 2011), pp. 105–6.

Is Morality Relative?

75 Lord Lammy, *The Victoria Climbié Inquiry* (Her Majesty's Stationery Office, 2003).

76 House of Commons Health Committee, *The Victoria Climbié Inquiry Report*, Sixth Report of Session 2002–3 (Her Majesty's Stationery Office, June 2003).

77 Homily of Joseph Cardinal Ratzinger, Dean of the College of Cardinals, Mass for the Election of the Supreme Pontiff, St Peter's Basilica, 18 April 2005, available at www.ewtn.com/pope/words/conclave_homily.asp.

78 Homily of his Holiness Benedict XVI, Bellahouston Park – Glasgow, 16 September 2010, www.vatican.va/holy_father/benedict_xvi.
79 Much of this chapter is adapted from Julian Baggini, 'Who's Afraid of Relativism?', *Dialogue*, 34, April 2010.

Without God, Is Everything Permitted?

80 Pope Benedict XVI, 'Spe Salvi' (Encyclical Letter), 30 November 2007, available at www.vatican.va/holy_father/benedict_xvi/encyclicals.
81 Pope Benedict XVI, 'Address of his Holiness Benedict XVI', Palace of Holyroodhouse, Edinburgh, 16 September 2010, available at www.vatican.va/holy_father/benedict_xvi/speeches.
82 William of Ockham, *Opera philosophica et theologica*, vol. 5, ed. Gedeon Gál et al. (The Franciscan Institute, 1967–8).
83 Thomas Nagel, *The View From Nowhere* (Oxford University Press, 1986), p. 5.

Can All Moral Dilemmas Be Resolved?

84 Joe Simpson, *Touching the Void* (Pan Books, 1989), pp. 86–7.
85 Isaiah Berlin, 'My Intellectual Path', in *The Power of Ideas* (Princeton University Press, 2001), pp. 1–23.
86 Isaiah Berlin, 'The Pursuit of the Ideal', *New York Review of Books*, Vol. 45, No. 8 (1998).
87 Berlin, 'My Intellectual Path', pp. 1–23.

Index